At the Paddock Gate

Horse stories for grown-ups

Jenny Roman

Cover Design by: www.itsawrapdesigns.com

For permission requests, email:
jennyroman-author@outlook.com

ISBN: 978-1-8381832-0-2

DEDICATION

This collection of short stories is for every horse mad grown-up who was once a ponyless, pony mad child. Oh, how we gazed enviously at every horse rider who rode by, and longingly at every pony we passed! Those of us who are now lucky enough to have horses in our lives will never forget the strength of that childhood longing.

Also By Jenny Roman

Fiction

The Camel in the Garden:
three short stories about loss, love and family

Beyond Words:
12 short stories about love, death and deception

And Not Forgetting Love:
12 short stories about love, mistakes and memories

Non-fiction

Short Story Competitions:
A Writer's Guide to Success

For more information, sign up for Jenny Roman's newsletter at:
http://bit.ly/JennyRomanNewsletter

CONTENTS

TERRIFIED TUESDAYS

She'd specifically said she was nervous, specifically said nothing too big. And they'd given her something the size of a Shire.

Archie, apparently. He was huge and brown with a roman nose and hooves the size of dinner plates. But after the initial shock, Steph found she was quite happy to stand holding him while she waited for the previous lesson to finish. He was placid enough, gazing over the fence at the other horses in the arena with disinterest, and taking the occasional sniff of Steph's pockets in the hope of a treat. After a while she plucked up enough courage to scratch him behind the ears, which he tolerated if not wholly enjoyed. The smell of horse took her straight back to her childhood, and she felt a surge of excitement and adrenaline.

She hadn't bothered to work out how long it had been since she'd last sat on a horse. Years. Decades actually. Life had got in the way. Specifically, Anton, who was the clean-living, urban type. He had allergies, so they couldn't have pets. Latterly, Steph had begun to wonder if the allergies weren't to do with domestic chores in general rather than merely the presence of pet hair. It wasn't that he actively stopped her going horse riding, it was more that it was easier to allow herself to be put off, to say it didn't fit in with their lifestyle, to say she would get round to it one day. Well, now Anton was gone, and this was the day.

When he'd first left (to move in with an uberchic urban girl from the office), Steph had experienced a devastating sense of loss. Slowly, this had morphed into resentment and anger. She had compromised so much about her life simply to fit in with Anton, and then he'd had the cheek to leave her. Eventually, she gave herself a mental shake. It should have been obvious to her long ago that she and Anton were incompatible. She reached the conclusion that he was much better off with his new mate, and she would be much better off avoiding men and sticking to horses.

Archie, gently nibbling her hair to check if it was in fact hay, clearly agreed.

In the arena, three children of between 8 and 12 years old were jumping a small course of coloured poles that looked colossal to Steph.

'Don't go getting ideas, buster,' she said to Archie. He turned his large brown eyes on her, and somehow managed to look slightly hurt. She glanced at the person standing next to her, hoping to share a grin, but the guy blanked her. 'Oops, clearly not amused!' she stage whispered. Archie flicked his ears at her in agreement.

The guy was slim and hunched into his jacket as though cold. In fact he didn't look at all well, with a slight pallor to his skin and bloodless lips. He seemed completely oblivious to Steph's presence. Not, thought Steph ruefully, that this was unusual in half-decent looking blokes. She sighed, and leant her head against Archie's warm neck. Horses. Stick to the horses.

In the arena, one of the ponies refused a jump. Its child rider tipped forward onto the pony's neck, and hung there for an agonising, drawn out moment, battling gravity, before the pony obligingly raised its head and the kid shuffled back down into the saddle, grinning.

The guy next to her turned away, his face now sickeningly sweaty.

'Not one of yours?' asked Steph kindly.

He looked startled. 'What?'

'The lass who almost came off.'

'Oh. No.' He glanced back at the arena for one last time, and then walked away towards the car park without another word.

'Well!' said Steph to Archie. 'Was it something I said?'

Steph watched the child pop the jump again with seemingly no fear, and this time the pony sailed over without putting a hoof wrong. The instructor decided this was a good point to draw the lesson to a close, and the riders gave their mounts a walk on a loose rein while the poles were packed away. Steph watched the clearance of the jumps with relief.

And then the children were sliding to the ground, and leading their ponies out, and it was Steph's turn. Without waiting for a signal, Archie stepped into the arena and plodded to the centre. Simultaneously, Steph's heart soared and her legs turned to jelly.

Even with the mounting block, it was a scramble onto Archie's broad back. While the instructor adjusted the stirrups, Steph gingerly took hold of the reins. Archie's solid neck was a comforting presence in front of her, and she could imagine grabbing his thick dark mane in an emergency. His first step forward took her by surprise, and for a moment her balance went, but then she tuned into the rhythm of his long, even stride, and suddenly she knew it would be fine. She could do this. A broad smile spread across her face.

The lesson was over all too soon, and the next group was heading into the arena. Walking back to the car park, Steph found she wanted to tell someone all about it, but there was only a girl mucking out and two mums chatting animatedly by the gate. She held the bubble of excitement and pride inside her. She'd done it! And she'd booked another lesson for Tuesday, her half day. She grinned to herself. In a way it was a shame Anton hadn't left a long time before.

When she arrived at the yard on Tuesday, it was almost deserted. After the bustle of the weekend, it was strange to see no-one in the arena, no queue of ponies awaiting the next lesson. The office was empty, so she walked across to the stables. In the distance, a figure stood by the fence, gazing at the ponies in the fields, shoulders hunched, hands in pockets. That guy again. Did he work here then? She turned away, not wanting to have to speak to him.

Archie stood in his box, head over his door, passively surveying the yard. She loved his wise expression, his calm brown eyes. But he wasn't tacked up. Had they forgotten she was coming?

She heard her name called, and glanced across the yard. Gail, the instructor, was with another horse on the opposite bank of stables.

'This is Fern,' said Gail. 'You did so well on old Archie the other day, I thought I'd put you on something a bit more challenging.'

A twist of fear lodged itself in Steph's stomach. 'I'm not sure I like the sound of "challenging"!'

'You'll be fine. I wouldn't put you on anything I didn't think you could handle. Archie's such a plod – great for learning the basics, but you don't need that.'

Fern was a bright bay with a neat black mane, and a flash of white running down her face. She was smaller and slighter than solid old Archie, but somehow Steph found this less comforting.

Astride Fern's wiry frame, Steph felt distinctly less safe. She said as much to Gail.

'She has much quicker strides,' said Gail. 'In fact, she's much more brisk about everything. But she's not nasty. She just wants to get on with the job. Keep nice and relaxed, and try to avoid the temptation to nag at her with your reins. She's not going to run off.'

But it didn't feel like that. Fern's choppy stride, her head bobbing energetically, reminded Steph of ponies she'd ridden as a child - the ones she'd tended to fall off. Steph was rigid with tension, and she could tell Fern was picking up on this. The horse kept cocking one ear back as if to say 'What's going on? What's worrying you? Should I be worried too?'

'Two things you need to do now,' said Gail, walking beside her.

'Go on?'

'Smile…'

Steph grimaced.

'…and breathe!'

'Oh, good point.' She had indeed been holding her breath. She let it out, feeling the tension release from her shoulders. Beneath her, Fern relaxed too, and the mare began to walk more freely, stretching her neck and shoulders, allowing Steph to sit deeper into the saddle. It was all suddenly much, much easier.

As she and Fern passed the gate, Steph was aware that the ill-looking guy was now standing watching. He still looked hunched and uncomfortable, but he appeared to be concentrating hard on her lesson.

'Who's that man?' Steph asked when they were at the other end of the arena again, out of earshot.

Gail glanced back. 'Oh, Ben. He's booked a lesson but he keeps cancelling. He...well, let's just say, he has some major anxiety issues. He's getting used to being around the yard, watching a few lessons, working up the courage to do it himself.'

Steph laughed grimly. 'Tell him not to watch me. I'm petrified too!'

'That might be a good thing,' said Gail. 'Now, come on, push her on into trot and we'll work on your balance and steering.'

It was going beautifully; Fern had relaxed, and they

were working well in circles and figures of eight. Then something must have spooked the ponies grazing out in the paddocks. Three of them threw up their heads and bolted to the far side of the field. Fern launched herself from collected trot into what felt to Steph like a flat out gallop. She lost a stirrup and lurched to one side, precariously.

'Sit up,' Gail called.

Steph gritted her teeth and held on. Fern reached the arena gate and stopped dead, snorting. Ben grabbed Fern's reins and for a moment, Steph, who had finished somewhere half up the horse's neck, was eyeball to eyeball with him. Weirdly, it was Ben who looked terrified. Steph gave him a sickly smile, and pushed herself back into the saddle, fishing carefully for her stirrups.

'Well sat!' she heard Gail call from behind.

Ben was still holding the reins, his knuckles white.

'Thanks,' said Steph, putting a hand soothingly on Fern's neck. 'She got a bit spooked there for a moment.'

Ben nodded.

'I think I'm OK now.' Steph glanced meaningfully at his hand on the reins.

He flushed, took his hand away and looked down.

'Thanks again.'

He said nothing. Steph could have sworn he was shaking.

She turned Fern back to the centre of the arena. 'Right, try again, shall we?'

'Sure you're OK?' asked Gail.

Steph was left with the sickly aftershock as the adrenaline ebbed away. If truth were told, she did feel a bit wobbly. But she'd stayed on. And she wasn't about to give up now.

The rest of the lesson went smoothly and afterwards she booked for the following Tuesday. When she left the office, Ben, hands in pockets, was watching a jumping lesson. On an impulse, she went straight up to him, determined to get at least an acknowledgement out of him.

'Ben?' she called boldly, smiling. 'Thanks for earlier. Who knows where I'd have ended up if you'd not grabbed her!'

Ben shook his head, not quite meeting her eye. 'You'd have been fine.'

'Maybe, maybe not. You've certainly got quick reflexes.'

He looked as if he was about to say something, but thought better of it. Instead, after a beat he said, 'You rode really well. Gail says it's only your second lesson.'

'Oh… I rode as a kid.' She shrugged. 'Only messing about, mind, at a scrappy local riding stables. It was all a bit rough and ready, not like this.' She waved an arm at the perfectly fenced and surfaced arena, the stables and paddocks. 'And there was no health and safety back then – we rode the ponies up from the field bareback and all sorts. But until last week, I'd not ridden for years.'

There was a pause. She waited for Ben to fill in some details of his own. He didn't.

'You're starting lessons here?' she prompted.

He shut his eyes for a moment, glanced up at the sky, took a breath and said, 'That's the plan.'

'Bit nervous?'

He gave a mirthless laugh. 'You could say that.'

'You'll be fine. Really.' She grinned at him. 'At the weekend when you saw me, I was terrified. If I can do it, anyone can.'

In the jumping paddock, one of the horses took an enormous leap over a spread fence, and swung close by where Steph and Ben were standing. She watched Ben take an unconscious step back. She didn't get it. Being nervous was one thing, but all his body language suggested he didn't even like horses.

'Have you been round the yard and met any of the horses?' she asked.

'No, I…'

'Come on then.' She set off towards the yard, and a moment later, heard him behind her.

She went straight to Archie's box. He looked over his door obligingly and nuzzled her hands. 'Has Gail said who you might ride? Maybe this lad?'

Ben came closer, took one hand out of his pocket and laid it on Archie's broad neck. The tiniest flicker of emotion crossed his face. Archie bent his head towards Ben's pockets.

'Nothing for you, lad.' Ben stepped back. 'Sorry.'

'I've got some mints if you want to give him one.' Steph fished a pack out of her coat.

Ben was saying, 'No, it's fine…' but already Steph had pressed a couple into his hand, and Archie was stretching his nose out eagerly. Steph watched Ben hold out a shaky hand, and the mint tumbled from his palm. Archie reached his nose over the stable door but couldn't stretch down far enough.

'Oops-ee,' said Steph, reaching down and popping the sweet back into Ben's palm. His hands were frozen. Maybe he *was* ill after all.

Ben held his hand out flat this time, and Archie accepted the treat politely, crunched and then demanded the second one.

'That's your lot,' said Ben, stroking a hand gently down Archie's wide face. He looked up at Steph, eyes brighter than she'd seen them before, and said, 'Thanks.'

'I've got plenty more.'

'Not for the mints.'

She grinned. 'You've got to start somewhere.'

'Yeah, I know.' He seemed to resolve something in his mind. He turned towards the office, and took a breath as if bracing himself. 'I'll go and book my first lesson – see you next week, eh?'

'Yes. See you.'

Steph watched him walking across the yard. He looked like a man going to the gallows.

When she arrived the following week, there was no sign of Ben. It was tipping down with rain and she had to run from the car to the yard. There were lights on in the indoor school. She went through the office and stealthily along the gangway to the viewing area. Archie stood in the centre of the arena, with Gail beside him. The portable mounting block was still to the left, and it appeared Ben had just got into the saddle. Steph glanced at her watch. She knew she was early, but it must have been at least a quarter of an hour into this half-hour slot. Fifteen minutes to pluck up the courage to mount?

She listened to the sound of the rain drumming on the roof, and watched the figure of Ben hunched over the front of the saddle, his hands wrapped in chunks of Archie's thick mane. Gail was obviously talking to him the whole time, but Steph couldn't hear what was being said. He made an attempt to sit up straighter. Archie shifted his weight slightly, resting a back leg, and Ben immediately hunched up again.

Gail turned, spotted Steph in the viewing area and beckoned her down.

'Would you hold Archie a minute while I just sort out Ben's stirrups?'

The idea of Archie needing to be held seemed laughable, but Steph took hold of his reins firmly without a word. She tried to smile up at Ben, but his eyes were fixed on Archie's neck, his jaw clenched, his skin covered with a sheen of sweat.

Steph remembered how nervous she had been when she'd first sat on Archie. What Ben was going through appeared to be a thousand times worse. What on earth was driving him to put himself through this?

Gail had adjusted the stirrup leathers, and was encouraging Ben to relax his lower leg and drop the weight into his heels. He began to sit up straight again.

'There, perfect!' said Gail, triumphant.

And he did look perfect. Like the pictures in the

textbooks. Only his glassy-eyed stare and the rigid way he was holding his shoulders gave him away.

'Now,' said Gail, never taking her eyes off Ben, 'Steph's going to walk on beside Archie, and I'm going to keep hold of your lower leg. If you feel wobbly, hook two fingers under the front of the saddle, but try not to tighten up that lower leg, or lean forward.'

Ben gave the slightest of nods.

'On we go then,' said Gail. Steph stepped forward, and Archie took his first lumbering stride. Ben shut his eyes for a moment, a wince of fear or pain crossed his face.

'You OK?' said Gail.

Ben nodded, opened his eyes and stared in front of him. They walked on maybe ten paces, then Gail said, 'OK, we're going to come to a halt now. Remember to sit deep into the saddle, keep your weight back and not let your upper body tip forward. Just think "halt" with your body.'

Steph stopped walking, and Archie stopped gently beside her. Ben let out a breath.

'OK, this time, we're still going to be walking with you,' said Gail, 'but you're going to make Archie walk on, and you're going to have to tell him when to stop.'

Steph saw Ben reach for the reins and settle them in between his fingers. Gail must have already gone through with him how to hold them properly. Archie bowed his head slightly to the contact and waited patiently for the instruction. Ben relaxed the reins, gave the slightest of squeezes with his legs and Archie walked forward smoothly. A few paces later, Ben shifted his weight slightly, and resisted a little with his reins. Archie stepped neatly to a halt.

'Spot on,' said Gail.

Ben looked down at them both, and grinned.

Ben stayed to watch Steph's lesson then afterwards they sat in the office, sipping coffee from the machine and watching the rain lashing against the windows.

'You've ridden before then?' asked Steph, her fingers wrapped around the cardboard cup.

'Like you, when I was a kid. Not for years. Didn't think I ever would again.'

'What made you decide to have another go?'

'Long story.'

Steph made a face to suggest she wasn't in a hurry.

'Let's just say, some things have changed for me recently. This is the first time I've had the opportunity.'

She waited for more, but evidently that was all Ben was willing to say.

'What about you?' he asked.

She told him about Anton, realising as she did so how much of a cliché it sounded. Hobby as a substitute for a relationship.

There was a silence. Then she said, 'I think you're really brave.'

He looked at her like she was mad. 'You're kidding! You saw me out there. Bricking it in walk.'

'That's what I mean. You were scared, but you did it anyway.'

'I watched you. Your first lesson that Saturday, and then last week. Saw how scared you were to begin with, and then when Fern bolted, you were scared, but you coped. I was scared *for* you and grabbed her, but then when I looked at you, I knew you were fine.'

Steph tried to remember if she'd felt fine. Afterwards, yes. But at the time? Had she known she was going to be alright?

'It sort of gave me a bit of a kick,' he went on. 'You could do it, why couldn't I?'

She grinned. 'And now you have.'

He nodded thoughtfully. 'Yeah. Now I have.'

'Maybe we could ask about sharing a lesson?' she suggested tentatively. 'Terrified Tuesdays!'

He tipped his head and blew out his cheeks,

considering. 'Hey, look, I don't want to hold you back.'

'Don't be silly. It'd be good – we'd give each other confidence. We'll have you trotting and cantering in no time, you'll see!'

He grinned back at her, and nodded, but his eyes were glassy and she knew he wasn't wholly convinced.

They talked to Gail, who suggested Ben have one more individual lesson, and then 'Terrified Tuesdays' began. Gail would use Steph on Fern as lead rider, and Ben would copy the exercises on Archie. Afterwards, they'd have a coffee, and Steph would try to think of something encouraging to tell Ben, or some useful piece of advice. Anything to make the next lesson easier. But it was very slow progress.

The first time she saw Ben trot, again Steph thought she saw a wince of pain, a stiffening of his back, but then he seemed to find Archie's rhythm, and everything fell into place. He and Archie practically floated around the arena. Steph was pretty impressed and gave him a thumbs up.

The first canter was much more difficult. For Steph, it felt like the natural next step and she was ready for it, but Ben seemed to have some kind of mental block. Even when he was theoretically giving the right signals for canter, his body language was all wrong, and Archie picked up on this. The safe old horse just trotted faster.

After yet another frustrating lesson, Steph said, 'You know, if you ever need to talk about anything – go through your anxieties or anything – well, I'd be happy to listen.' She pulled out her mobile phone. 'Swap numbers? Just in case?'

She watched him hesitate, and for a moment wondered if she'd read it all wrong. Was he with someone? He never said much about his home life, his background. In some ways she hardly knew anything about him, and yet in others – witness to the painful conquering of his fear – she knew him inside out.

Just as she was feeling a flush of embarrassment creep up her neck, he pulled out his own phone and grinned. 'Yeah, that'd be great.'

As she tapped in his number, a tingle of excitement ran down her spine. Her first thought was to scold herself for being adolescent, but she dismissed it immediately. It was a fantastic feeling. After all those stale years with Anton, she deserved it.

They began to talk on the phone – sporadically at first, and only about horse-related topics – Steph passing on info about confidence-boosting techniques, or courses she'd read about. Gradually though, their conversations broadened, and they fell into a pattern of talking in the evenings. It appeared to be helping. Ben was evolving into a different person; he'd got past the barrier in his head and could now canter with ease. In fact, he now looked more comfortable and confident in the saddle than Steph, which secretly Steph found annoying. She herself needed to pick up some extra tips from somewhere.

She decided to dig out all her old pony books from her teenage years which had been tucked away in the loft gathering dust. Dust and spiders, as it turned out. There were boxes and boxes of books and creased magazines. The sight of them, titles wholly alien to people like Anton, made her realise just how much of herself she had buried whilst in her old relationship.

She began to leaf through the yellowing pages of the magazines, grinning at all the old photos of her favourite show jumpers. It brought back so many memories. And then she turned a page and frowned. A black and white photo of a guy standing between two stunning horses, their bridles plastered with rosettes. It was Ben. She mentally shook herself. Of course it wasn't Ben. The man in the picture was older, maybe in his early fifties. She flipped to the cover of the magazine. It was dated October 1995. She turned back to the photograph. Underneath the caption read "Jimmy Townley with two of his stable's top jumpers at this year's Horse of the Year Show". Beneath, was an article about the Townley yard, which Jimmy had built from scratch and which was still very much a family affair. Daughter Vicky rode the top flight horses, whilst the young stock was brought on by son Ben.

She grabbed another issue of the magazine, and then another, flicking through the results pages. Time and time again, Ben's name was listed in the top three at jumping competitions all around the country. There was even a photograph of him accepting a cup from Lady somebody-or-other. An incredibly young version of the Ben she knew; painfully slight, a determined yet haunted looking boy.

Steph sat back on her heels feeling the blood drain from her face. He'd been a professional rider! All those times she'd thought she was showing him how to do something. All the times she'd encouraged him, all the tips she'd given him. She felt sick with shame. She'd had a handful of lessons as a kid, a few weeks in the summer mucking about in some down-at-heel stables in her home town, while he'd been competing on the national circuit! How could he not have said something? How could he have let her make such a fool of herself?

She rang the riding school and cancelled her lesson, making some excuse about not feeling well. The thought of missing her weekly ride was awful, but she couldn't face Ben. It would be too humiliating.

On Tuesday afternoon, she tried to keep herself busy in the house. Just before their lesson was due to start, her mobile rang, and Ben's name appeared on the screen. She switched on the vacuum cleaner to drown it out, and he didn't try again.

She vacuumed everywhere, despite the fact some of the rooms didn't really need doing, and then set about cleaning the bathroom. Anything to avoid thinking about Ben. She was fed up with men turning out to be something other than they'd seemed.

When there was nothing left to clean, she sat in the kitchen with a cup of coffee.

And that's when the doorbell went.

'Just what I need,' she muttered, 'someone selling double glazing or religion!'

It was Ben, holding a bunch of flowers.

'Gail said you were under the weather. I was worried.' He gazed at her face. 'Are you OK?'

She stalked back into the house, heard him come in behind her, and close the door after him.

'Steph?'

She picked up the magazine, folded back at the page containing his teenage photo.

'Were you ever going to mention this?'

He took the magazine, blew out his cheeks and said, 'Oh. That.'

'Yes, that. The being-a-professional-rider thing. The "my dad's Jimmy Townley, the famous producer of top class show jumpers" thing. Had you forgotten?'

Ben sighed. 'I've tried to over the years.'

'I can see how it would be a terrible burden,' said Steph sarcastically.

Ben bit his lip. He closed the magazine and glanced at the front cover. 'Don't happen to have an issue from, say, January 1996, do you?'

'No idea,' said Steph. 'Why? Did it report your win at Olympia or something?'

He began to flick through the pile of magazines, turned some pages, and then presented her with a bland page of text.

'What am I supposed to be looking at exactly?'

'Third column, near the bottom.'

She took the magazine, and read down the page. Phrases jumped out at her. ..shocking accident...Ben Townley schooling at home...broken pelvis, shattered left leg…possible difficulty walking… She looked up. 'Oh my God, Ben.'

'That's kind of why I didn't mention it.'

The thought of him, smashed up, in agony, brought tears to her eyes. Without thinking, she threw her arms around him. He stood, stiffly, unmoving for a moment, then his arms came cautiously around her. A shuddering relief swept over her.

After a moment she pulled away. 'How long did it take to recover?'

'Difficult to say really. They had to pin what was left of me together. Then some of the breaks didn't set right and they had to start over. I'd get a bit better, start learning to walk again, and then I'd be knocked back another couple of months.'

Steph winced. 'And of course you couldn't ride again. You must have been devastated.'

'No, I was relieved.'

Steph looked blankly at him.

'The horse I'd come off was a youngster. One of the hundreds and hundreds of half-wild, lunatic horses my dad bought in dirt cheap because no-one else would touch them. He'd get me to start them off, knock the worst of the bad behaviour out of them, take them to a few shows, and sell them on. The decent ones always went to Vicky. Then I'd start over with a new batch. OK, I had one bad fall, but actually I'd just been lucky up to then. I could have had an accident just as bad – or worse – practically every day.

'So when I woke up in hospital, I thought, 'Thank God, I don't have to ride for a bit.' Of course, neither of us knew how bad it was for a while. Dad kept asking the doctors how long before I could ride again. They looked at him like he was mad. Well, I suppose he was. I made a decision while I was lying there in agony, waiting for the next batch of painkillers, that I'd never ride for him again. And frankly, by the time I got back home, even the sound of hooves, or something silly like the clink of a girth buckle, would make me feel sick. I never wanted to get on a horse ever again.'

'So, what changed your mind?' asked Steph.

Ben took a breath. 'Dad died last year. Because Vicky got the yard, I got the lion's share of the money. Suddenly I didn't have to work all hours. And I spent a lot of time thinking. I'd stopped riding because my dad had forced me to ride. But deep down I still *wanted* to ride - just something that wasn't half-wild! So I booked a lesson. But when I got to the riding school, I couldn't face it. Just seeing horses again made me feel sick. It'd taken weeks of hanging around almost every day just to get to the stage where I could stand by the arena and watch other people riding. And that's when you turned up.'

'Thinking I knew it all! Trying to give you advice!'

'Not at all – you were great. That moment with the mints...' He smiled suddenly, reached forward and put his hands on her shoulders, thumbs against her collarbones. 'I couldn't have done it without you. I almost didn't ride this afternoon when I realised you weren't there.'

'Sorry. I just felt so stupid. And I was furious you'd not said something. But of course, now it's obvious why.' She gave him a watery smile. 'I'll be there next week, promise.'

Ben looked at her steadily. 'I'm kinda hoping you'll be there always,' he said softly.

THE FOREVER FIELD

I stared at the three wheelbarrows in the glare of the floodlight and felt the rage mounting within me. The green metal one, which had been fine yesterday, now had a spongy flat tyre. The purple plastic one (everyone's favourite) had been abandoned right next to the muck heap, containing a heaped load of stinking deep litter bed. This left the rusty brown one with the squeaky wheel which everyone avoided. It was full of putrid pooey rainwater.

'That's it!' I muttered under my breath. 'I've had enough.'

It's funny how it's the little things which get to you. I'd had a long day at work. I was late getting to the yard. It was dark and cold, and all I wanted to do was get home and enjoy a glass of wine and something to eat. Before that I had to muck out, but somehow all the shavings forks had mysteriously disappeared (except the little pink one Kirsty had bought for her nine year old daughter), and the only broom in evidence was the one where the head fell off every third or fourth sweep. The wheelbarrows were the final straw (no pun intended - I was definitely beyond puns).

I mucked out in record time, despite the diminutive fork, the whole time muttering to myself that I needed to find a new livery yard and, at the same time, feeling guilty because Kirsty, the owner, was absolutely lovely but never had any time to deal with any of the problems around the yard. It was rapidly becoming the worst livery yard I'd ever been on.

To be fair, the place had looked really promising when I'd first enquired about bringing Murphy. I'd had my lovely old black cob for ten years and he'd given me bucket loads of confidence during our time together. At our previous yard, we'd done all the activities, jumping, dressage, even a cross-country course, not to mention fun rides and the occasional show. But he was 23 now and it was time for him to slow down a bit. I'd wanted to find a quieter place where he could enjoy grazing in the field with a few pony pals, and we could potter out for the odd hack. When Kirsty had shown me around, the stables were smart and roomy, and the paddocks well fenced. Best of all, there were no turnout restrictions. But that had been last April. Now it was January, and we'd had one of the wettest winters on record. The paddocks had turned into the Somme, and the gateways were like bogs.

None of this would have been a problem if everyone had tidied up after themselves, but of course with less daylight and the vile weather, the liveries were skimping on any non-essential tasks, so the whole place was descending into chaos. And of course, Kirsty was too nice to have a go at anyone about it, and too busy to do anything about it herself. And her husband, who viewed the livery yard as his wife's "little hobby" was about as much use as a chocolate fireguard. He himself was not interested in the horses or the yard at all, in fact he merely seemed to regard it all as a bit of an inconvenience. If it had been my husband, Darren, every sagging strand of electric fence would have been re-strung, the hinges re-aligned on every drooping gate, and the arena surface levelled every day.

I sighed, and wheeled the horrible squeaky wheelbarrow to the muck heap. I had hoped to soon be in a position to buy another horse and properly retire Murphy. (Of course, he'd have a forever home with me, but I longed for a new horse to bring on too.) So what I really needed was somewhere cheaper where I could afford to keep two beasties. But standing on that muck heap, my heart plummeted into my shavings-encrusted wellies, because I knew I wasn't going to be able to find this mythical place. I knew because I'd already looked. Of course I'd looked! That's what I did in the evenings - scrolled through lovely pictures of beautiful green pastures on my phone, and wished. There were no other yards as close as Kirsty's place. Further afield, any decent ones would have added a lengthy commute to my already long day, or were well beyond my limited budget.

I tried to ignore the voice in my head that said my budget might not have been so limited if I'd gone for that promotion at work. If I'd not chickened out of applying at the last minute. If I'd not convinced myself I couldn't do it, and so allowed someone with less experience to step smoothly into the role, unchallenged. Grr!

Grabbing Murphy's headcollar, I stomped off down to the field to fetch him in. I couldn't decide if I was more annoyed with Kirsty, the other liveries, the weather, or the general unfairness of life. But as I traipsed through the mud, I knew deep down the person I was most annoyed with was me.

Darren was already home when I pulled onto the drive. The kitchen light was on, and the room looked gloriously warm and inviting through the window.

'Hey!' I called, as I backed into the house, pulling off my wellies. I hung up my coat, threw down my bag, and said, 'What a bloody day!'

Darren was sitting at the kitchen table. His eyes were unfocused.

'What's up?' I slid into the seat opposite. 'Sweetheart?'

Without looking at me, he took a letter which had been resting on the table in front of him, and spun it towards me. Even before I'd picked it up, the word 'redundancy' jumped out at me. I read the letter and looked up at him. This time his eyes met mine, and he looked totally defeated.

'Fourteen years,' was all he said.

'How has this - ?' I stopped. 'I mean, they can't - just like that, out of the blue?'

'It's not out of the blue,' said Darren with a sigh. 'There've been rumours for months.'

This new information knocked the wind out of me for a moment. 'You never said.'

Darren shrugged. 'They were just rumours. I didn't want to worry you.'

'But we could have been more careful at Christmas.'

Nausea rose within me. All those festive purchases were tainted now.

'Zoe, we didn't go mad. And hey, if it was our last decent Christmas, at least we enjoyed it without worrying.'

The cold claw of panic was stealing over me. Darren was being made redundant. There would be just one income coming into the household. It wouldn't be enough to cover the mortgage and all the bills. We'd lose the home that we'd created together. Words jumbled in my brain: repossession, bankruptcy. What about Murphy? I'd never be able to afford the livery now. How stupid that just an hour ago all I'd been worried about was a bloody wheelbarrow!

I sighed, picked up the letter again and read it over. 'OK, so they're giving you three months' notice. So we've got some time to work out what to do. And you'll get a redundancy payment - it says here they'll send you a quote in a separate letter.'

'Not expecting it to be much above the statutory,' said Darren. He pushed his hands through his hair. 'It's so stupid, I can't believe it. The longer people kept talking about it... Well, you get so used to hearing the talk, you don't believe it will ever happen.'

'I wish you'd said something earlier.'

Darren shrugged. 'Like I said, it wasn't real. Just a standing joke around the office. And I'd even started thinking perhaps it's for the best. You know, I'd never leave if I wasn't pushed, I'm too comfortable, even though it's hardly the job of my dreams. Maybe it would give me the kick I need. Bit of redundancy - I could set up something on my own. But now it's actually happened, I'm petrified.' He looked up at me. 'What am I going to do?'

I got up, went round the table and threw my arms around him. 'It's not what *you're* going to do, it's what *we're* going to do. Whatever we have to put in place to get through this, we'll work it out together. Alright?'

I felt him nodding into my shoulder.

And although my heart was still thumping against my chest, I knew I had to be strong for Darren, because my normally big brave husband was freaking out.

That night, I lay in bed, sleep refusing to come. I stared blankly into the darkness, and listened to the familiar sounds of the house around me; the gentle tick of the radiators cooling now the heating had gone off. The distant hum of the fridge. The almost imperceptible electronic buzz of Darren's old alarm clock. All this familiarity was now suddenly at risk. I didn't doubt Darren would find another job, but what if it wasn't as good? What if his commute got longer, or we had to move? Adrenaline coursed through me, my body preparing for a fight my brain couldn't work out. The bedclothes stuck to my sweaty skin.

Beside me, Darren rolled over and sighed.

'You awake too?' I whispered.

'What do you think?'

'Want a cup of tea?'

Darren grunted.

I swung myself out of bed and padded out onto the landing, pausing by the window and staring out at the garden bathed in moonlight. In my pony books as a child, often the heroine had kept her pony in the back garden, turning the garage into a stable. I imagined keeping Murphy on our tiny square of lawn. Assuming we could have squeezed him through the side gate, he'd have trodden it to mud within the hour. And we didn't have a garage.

Life was not like fiction.

By the time I'd returned with the tea, Darren had given up on trying to sleep and turned on the bedside lamp. I grabbed a notepad and pen, and said, 'Right, this is silly. There's no point lying here worrying. We need a plan of action - otherwise we're both just going to be staring at the ceiling all night.'

Darren closed his eyes with a groan.

'Come on. We can work this out.' I tapped the pen against my teeth. 'So first things first, how long can we keep going as we are on one salary?'

'With the redundancy payment - assuming it's not much better than statutory?' Darren paused a moment. 'Four or five months? Six maybe, if we're careful.'

'That should give you enough time to get another job, shouldn't it?'

Darren shrugged. 'I guess. But that's the thing, you don't know, do you? What if I can't? And even if I do land something, it's not likely to be on as good money as I'm getting now.'

'So we need to start cutting back, to eke out the redundancy as long as possible, and to be able to afford you taking a drop in salary. We need to make a list of all our outgoings, and work out what to cut back on.'

My eyes met Darren's over the notepad.

Darren put his hand on my arm. 'I'd never ask you to get rid of Murphy - you know that, don't you? He's part of the family.'

I threaded my fingers through his, and squeezed. 'I know, I know. That's why I married you!'

We gave each other watery grins, and unlinked fingers. I opened the banking app on my phone and started to scroll through the payments. Neither of us had stuff which might have been easy to give up, like gym memberships we didn't use. My car, though old, was purchased outright but Darren's was on Finance which was a fairly hefty amount.

'Could we manage with only one car?' I asked.

Darren made a face.

'Or buy one second hand?' I scribbled a note for myself. 'We'll get in touch with the Finance company tomorrow and ask them how much it will cost to come out of the deal.'

Buoyed up by this potential saving, I carried on looking down the list, but every other payment coming out of our account was for depressingly necessary stuff. The mortgage was a terrifying amount. After that and all the utilities, there was the broadband and the phones, and food. OK, so I'd get on the price comparison sites over the weekend, and maybe we could shave some money off our payments.

But that didn't change the obvious. My fingernail rested against one figure on the screen. Despite what we'd just agreed, the other single biggest payment that jumped out was Murphy's livery bill.

The feeling of nausea was back.

People say that things always look better in the morning, but that's a load of bollocks. When I got to the yard to turn out, there was a brown envelope stuck behind the name plate of each stable door. Murphy had dribbled on his, but the bill was still a bill. Worse, it included the extra fees for a weekend of full livery over New Year when we'd stayed over at Darren's sister's, plus the cost of wormer and the farrier, as well as all the usual winter hay.

A couple of the other girls were tacking up to ride out and asked if I wanted to join them, but I wasn't in the mood. I turned Murphy out, mucked out, and then headed to the supermarket to do the food shop. All the way round I found myself putting the cheapest brand in the trolley, or talking myself out of purchases.

It was starting to rain again when I came out of the supermarket, and I realised I'd forgotten to get a birthday card for Darren's niece, so I dumped all the shopping in the car, and jogged up the ally way to the high street. I was heartily wishing I'd remembered my brolly, which was still in the car, when the rain went from being mildly annoying to a positive monsoon. I scurried into the nearest shop doorway, hunched into my coat, and glanced in the window. It was an estate agents. Pictures of beautiful detached homes stared back at me, with eye-watering prices. There was a gorgeous old farm house with three acres which looked absolutely stunning, but it came with a price tag with a disturbing number of digits. I turned to the other side of the doorway and looked in that window. Ah, this was clearly the more realistic end of the housing spectrum. Here was a range of flats and starter homes, some budget new builds, a pretty but tiny barn conversion, and then I spotted a couple of semis similar to ours. I looked at the asking prices. If they were realistic, it was satisfying to think there was a bit of equity in our place. If we needed to re-mortgage, that would be in our favour.

When I got home, Darren was sitting in the lounge, laptop propped on his knees, gazing at the screen.

'Any luck?' I asked, dumping the shopping in the hall, and going in to kiss him on the cheek.

'I've registered on a few job sites. Spotted a couple of things I could go for.'

'That's good.'

'Yeah, me and all the other guys who are losing their jobs!' he said grimly.

'But you're better than all the other guys.'

Darren made a face. 'I think you're biased.' He turned the screen towards me. 'But *you* might like this one.'

I peered at the screen. The role sounded pretty similar to the one I'd talked myself out of applying for at my place - only the money was significantly better.

He nudged the curser towards a line part way down the ad. 'Look, they specifically mention that some of the work can be done from home - so even though it's a bit further away, you'd probably be able to cut down on your overall weekly commute.'

I studied the ad a bit more carefully. It was definitely interesting. Recently I'd been giving some thought to attempting to reduce my hours. Obviously that was looking like a pipe dream with Darren's redundancy on the horizon, but some flexibility with homeworking would be the next best thing.

'Looks like I'll have to blow the dust off my CV after all!' I said.

'You and me both!' said Darren ruefully.

When I woke on Sunday, the sun was actually shining.

'Going out for a ride?' asked Darren, sleepily.

'I'd like to spend some time with you - I'll go and turn out and come home.'

Darren pushed himself up on his pillows. 'Na. I'll come with you. I'll chuck my bike in the car and cycle out with you and Murphy.'

I grinned at him. We'd not done that in years.

About an hour later, Murphy and I were heading down the road from the livery yard, with Darren a little way ahead on his bike. It was a bit tricky to hold a proper conversation, so we had degenerated into singing silly songs. To begin with, there hadn't been too much traffic about, but as we went on, an increasing number of cars began to overtake us and I was looking forward to turning off up our usual track to the left. When we reached it though, we discovered the recent wet weather had turned it into a bog. It wasn't going to be much fun for me and Murphy, and it would be practically impossible for Darren on the bike.

'There's a lane on the left, a bit further up,' I suggested, as we hesitated by the muddy track. I glanced around, worried for Murphy's round backside in the stream of traffic. 'It'll take us a bit out of the way, so it'll make for a longer ride, but at least it'll be solid ground.'

'Sounds like a better bet,' said Darren, pedalling onwards.

I put Murphy into a steady trot and we followed Darren along the road and up to the turn off for the lane, leaving the traffic behind. Murphy gratefully dropped back to a walk, gave three grunts and an enormous snort.

'There's a good lad,' I said, giving him a pat. 'That's better, isn't it?'

'I know how he feels!' said Darren, who was also breathing heavily. 'That bit was more uphill than it looked.' He glanced at Murphy. 'It's alright for her, isn't it, mate? She's just sat there - it's me and thee doing all the work!'

I stuck my tongue out at him.

After the busy road, it was lovely riding along the lane. Murphy's hooves clopped on the tarmac, and Darren weaved beside us on the bike, finding it harder to cycle slowly despite his complaints about the previous faster pace. From Murphy's broad back, I could see over some of the hedges and gates to a collection of pretty cottages, and then the cottages gave way to open fields, then some woodland. I was just thinking that Murphy and I should use this route more often when my usually bombproof pony spooked and jumped sideways.

'Whoa!' said Darren, who had to swerve out of the way, and almost ended up in the hedge on the far side of the lane. 'What was all that about? He never shies at anything!'

I patted Murphy's neck, collected up my reins and nodded ahead of us. 'It's that piece of board, lying in the road by that gateway.'

Darren wobbled over to the gateway, got off his bike and leaned it against the gate.

'It's a For Sale board,' he said, gently picking it up.

Murphy snorted and ran back a couple of steps. I could feel the tension in his body through the saddle. 'Bless you - it's not going to eat you, you daft thing. Daddy will beat it into submission!'

The board was attached to a stake which had snapped near the bottom.

'Must have got knocked by someone using the gateway as a pull-in.' Darren wedged it into the hedge. Then he paused and looked over the gate. 'Do you think this is what's for sale - this field?'

'Must be.'

I rode Murphy closer to the gate and we looked over. It was a nice sized field - about three or four acres - bounded by a big hedge. There was a dilapidated wooden barn off to the left behind the hedge, and some tall trees at the bottom.

'Shame there's no stables,' said Darren. 'Wonder how much it is.'

'It'll be for auction,' I said. 'Land always is.'

'Doesn't say so on the board. I'll look it up.' Darren pulled his phone from his pocket, tapped the screen and frowned. 'Oh, no signal!'

'I wouldn't worry. It'll be a development site - going for millions.'

'Nah,' Darren looked up and down the lane. 'There's no other buildings here - there were those cottages way back, but this is just grazing land.'

'Well, if it's going for more than three hundred and eighty-six quid, I'm afraid we can't afford it,' I said ruefully, thinking of the current total in our joint account.

'Nice thought though, isn't it?' said Darren. 'Having your own place.'

I gazed over the gate and nodded. I could feel my heart swelling with the idea. Yes, it was a lovely thought. Shame it could only be a dream right now.

My best skirt was feeling a tiny bit tight. Still, it looked the part, and that's what mattered. First impressions and all that. Darren and I had been swotting up on interview techniques over the past few weeks. He'd been for a couple, got called back for a second round at one place, but ultimately didn't get it. Still, he was feeling better for having got back 'out there'.

As for me, I felt like a kid on her first day at school. My palms were sweaty, and my neatly ironed blouse was already creased from the car journey over. I tried to remind myself that I was a professional. I could do this.

A woman appeared at the door of the room where I'd been asked to wait.

I looked up expectantly, ready to get to my feet, but she gave me a big smile and said, 'Ever so sorry - we're running a bit behind. The Managing Director was held up first thing this morning, and it's knocked the schedule out. So sorry to keep you waiting.'

'Oh, no problem.' I'd told work I had a dentist appointment - hinted that there was likely to be some nasty procedure required, so I wouldn't be missed if it took a bit longer.

'Thank you so much for your patience!' the woman beamed at me. 'Can I get you anything - a tea or coffee perhaps?'

I shook my head. 'Very kind of you, but no, I'm fine thanks.' I gave her a big smile back. I'd already had about ten wees that morning. It wasn't worth the risk.

Darren had been priming me with interview questions all weekend, so since there was no need to do any last minute cramming, I got my phone out and decided to look up the ad for that field we'd seen for sale. The search engine on the agents' website wasn't exactly intuitive, but finally I found it. Not silly money at all, actually. I tapped my nails against my teeth. The thing was, if we had our own land, I wouldn't be shelling out for livery every month. In fact, I might be able to get a paying livery of my own.

I began to imagine it as a little yard, divided up into paddocks, the barn refurbished, perhaps a couple of stables or a field shelter.

The woman appeared at the door. 'We're ready for you now, if you'd like to come through.'

I jumped to my feet, dreams scattering in all directions. The interview! I needed to focus on the interview!

A slim, glamorous woman stood to greet me as I went into the room. My heart sank. She looked the consummate professional - perfect tailored suit, not a hair out of place, scarily high heels.

'Zoe,' she said warmly, 'I'm Nicola Graham. So sorry to keep you waiting - had a bit of a crisis this morning.'

'No problem at all,' I said, concentrating on making my voice level and calm. 'Hope it's been resolved?'

'Well, fingers crossed.' Nicola crossed two perfectly manicured fingers. 'Had to have the vet out to my horse this morning - colic.'

'Oh my God, it's terrifying, isn't it?' I said without thinking. 'So awful seeing them so distressed - happened to mine a couple of years ago.'

'You have horses too?' said Nicola, sitting down and leaning forward conspiratorially over the desk which separated us. 'Fantastic! You'd not believe it, but there's not another soul here who rides - it's absolutely deadly. What a breath of fresh air you will be!'

'So, how did it go?' Darren came into the kitchen, his head tipped to one side as if trying to work out from my expression whether it was good news or bad.

'Oh,' I said, airily. 'Got the job.'

'What? That's fantastic!' said Darren.

'Yup, I can work from home some of the time - I only need to go in for meetings and specific training etc.'

Darren picked me up and spun me round.

'Oh, and we've got the estate agents coming round at the weekend,' I went on.

'What? Why?'

'To value the house.'

Darren put me down and gazed at me. 'Zoe, don't be mad. You've just landed a better job. I'll get something soon. We'll be able to make the mortgage. You love this place.'

I looked around at the house that had been our home for the last 12 years. 'Yes, I do. But it's just a building.' I pulled him into my arms. 'I love *you* more, you and Murphy, and our life together. I don't want us to be under so much pressure to pay the mortgage that we're making ourselves miserable. We could manage with a smaller house, couldn't we?'

'Yes, but is that really what you want?'

'I want us to be able to live. I want to be able to spend the evenings with you, not have you coming home from work late, so exhausted you just want to veg in front of the telly. I want you to have the time and energy and cash to be able to go and play a round of golf, or go fishing or whatever you want to do.'

'That sounds nice,' said Darren ruefully.

'And besides...' I paused. 'I was wondering about using the equity.'

Darren frowned. 'How do you mean?'

'I looked up the ad for that grazing land we passed the other day.'

Darren burst out laughing. 'All that bollocks about me going golfing and fishing! You want to buy a field!'

I grinned back at him. 'Maybe!'

Murphy's hooves clopped evenly on the tarmac of the lane. On either side, the hedges danced in the autumn breeze, and a pale sun shone across the distant fields. A huge grin spread across my face. There was nothing like the simple pleasure of pottering out on good old Murphy. And to be honest, now we'd got our mojo back and were going out more regularly, the old boy was much keener and we were really starting to explore more.

We came to the gate, and Murphy shied. It had become a little ritual, even though the For Sale board was long gone.

'Silly sod,' I said. 'This is your home now, remember?'

I kicked my feet out of the stirrups, slid to the floor and opened the gate. There was a whinny from somewhere to the left.

'Hello, baby girl,' I called to the chestnut filly. She stood with her head thrown up, as close to the electric fence as she could get. She whinnied again as we walked in and shut the gate. Murphy gazed at her impassively. I rubbed his nose and whispered, 'I know she's a bit daft at the moment, but you'll get to love her one day, honest.' Murphy gave a sigh as if he doubted it, and rubbed his head against my chest.

I'd just turned him out when there was the sound of a car in the lane. Darren pulled into the gateway in the old hatchback he'd found in the bargain ads.

He climbed out and leaned over the gate. 'Nice ride?'

'Lovely, thanks.' I planted a kiss on his lips. 'How did you get on this morning?'

'Woman came for the big sofa as arranged - so that's gone. And I'm taking the coffee table to that bloke I spoke to this morning.' Darren nodded at the back of the car where the seats were folded down, and the too-large coffee table was wedged in.

'So that's the lot?' I grinned.

'Yup - we are now officially minimalist in our bijou home!'

'Wow. That feels amazing.'

And it really did. Like an enormous weight had been lifted from our lives. It wasn't as though we'd gone from a mansion to a hovel, but scaling down from our three bed house with separate dining room, to a two bed with a kitchen-diner had meant being really disciplined about what furniture we were keeping and what we were getting rid of. At the beginning, it had been painful to part with stuff, but in the end, we realised that's all it was - stuff. And stuff wasn't as important to us as living our lives in the way we wanted.

'Feels like a proper new beginning, doesn't it?' said Darren.

And it really was. Darren had taken on some consultancy work for a couple of months and was enjoying not having a specific 9-to-5 job for the moment. The money I was saving on livery, I was putting to the new mortgage, and what with my pay rise, we could afford for him to have the odd break from work. The difference in him was incredible.

'Well, it might not be our forever home,' I said. 'But it's perfect for now.'

We watched Murphy go down and roll, give himself a shake, and wander over to the chestnut filly to graze.

'Yeah, true, it might not,' Darren said. 'But I think this might be our forever field.'

ONE IN A MILLION

The light from the head torch was fading. Drew, picking his way carefully down the muddy track, wondered how long the batteries were supposed to keep going. When would Caroline have last replaced them? He felt the usual sharp stab at the thought of her, but pushed it away.

It was so bloody dark. And all the other horses were in. It was just poor old Siegfried left out in the paddock. Why did the department progress meeting have to overrun today of all days? Usually Gemma, the yard owner, brought all the horses in on weeknights, but at the beginning of the week she'd reminded all the liveries that on Friday night they would have to make arrangements to bring in their own horses as she was going out. At the time Drew had read the message, it had just been a minor inconvenience in a week packed with project deadlines and other seemingly insurmountable tasks, but now he knew what a pain in the arse it was going to be.

His foot slipped in the mud and he cursed. Why hadn't he remembered his bloody wellies? He'd found an old pair of trainers in the back of the car which he'd pulled on to replace his work shoes, but he'd not counted on the heavy rain they'd had earlier that day which had made the path treacherous. Siegfried was standing right by the gate, his head thrown up, the whites of his eyes showing in the beam from Drew's head torch. There was a gust of wind, Drew slipped again, the head torch bobbed, and Siegfried snorted, wheeled round and galloped off into the darkness.

'Oh, don't be a dick!' Drew shouted into the night. He squelched up to the gate, pulled back the latch and slipped through, shutting it behind him quickly. The mud was deeper on this side of the gate where Siegfried had been stomping around. Drew's foot went into a hole and freezing muddy water sloshed into his trainer. He swore again.

There was the sound of hooves, and Siegfried reappeared at a trot, goggling at the beam from the head torch and slithering to a halt a few feet off.

'Come on, mate,' said Drew, keeping his voice calm in the way Caroline had always done, 'Let's get you out of this bloody weather, eh?'

Siegfried blew hard through flared nostrils, and took a couple of steps closer before halting again. Drew pulled his foot out of the mud and went up to Siegfried, slowly, keeping the beam of the head torch pointed to the ground. He got the headcollar over Siegfried's nose and was just about to flip the strap over the back of his head when Siegfried threw his head up, whacking Drew in the face. Drew dropped the headcollar, tried to step back out of the way, but the sodden ground sucked at his trainers. Before he knew it, he was standing in the mud in his socks.

In the stable, Siegfried became the placid beast Drew always remembered seeing with Caroline. The dark bay gelding pulled contentedly at his haynet and regarded Drew with calm brown eyes as though he had not danced and pulled like a racehorse all the way up the path from the field, had not seen gremlins in every glistening puddle, and had not heard demons in every gust of wind.

'What was all that about?' said Drew, leaning over the

stable door and examining his hands - they were filthy, and there was a mild rope-burn across his right palm. In the reclaimed trainers, the cold mud still oozed between his toes. 'It wasn't my fault I was late - I told you, the meeting overran. I kept saying I had to go, but you know how it is. Well, actually, you probably don't - you're a horse.' Drew paused. 'So it's come to this. I'm talking to a horse.'

Siegfried took a step towards the door, stuck out his nose, and sniffed Drew's coat hopefully.

'You've got your hay, what more do you want?' said Drew in mock outrage.

Siegfried blew gently over Drew's hands, the breath warm on his icy fingers. Drew rubbed the white blaze on Siegfried's face affectionately. 'You're a daft sod, you are. Do you miss your mum? Yeah? Well, I miss her too.'

Drew's eyes misted.

'Gotta go, mate. Thanks to you my bloody feet are freezing!'

The house was dark and silent. He'd still not got used to that - the way the place was always exactly how he'd left it. There were some envelopes on the mat, including some junk mail addressed to Caroline which he stuck straight in the recycling. His days were full of these tiny, insignificant hurts. Seeing her name, or her handwriting on something, or hanging up his coat and getting a sudden waft of her perfume from an old scarf on the next coat hook. Sometimes the pain was almost comforting. It reminded him that at one time he had felt something for someone. Not just this fog of grey nothingness.

He heated up a ready meal in the microwave, grabbed a plate, and plonked his dinner on the kitchen table. It was Friday night. He could have a glass of wine with his crappy dinner, but something stopped him. He knew he'd been drinking a little too much in recent weeks. Of course, it was excusable, but it was a slippery slope. And besides, if he was honest with himself, it didn't really help.

He sat down to eat, remembered the mail, and tore open the first envelope. His credit card bill. The total was alarming. How had things got this bad?

This is what people forgot, he mused, that when you lost your partner, you didn't just have to deal with your grief. There was all the practical stuff too - and money was the worst.

He looked at the total to pay, and knew he needed to speak to Gemma in the morning.

The yard was Saturday-busy. Kids and ponies milling around, the scrape and clunk of stables being mucked out, a couple of horses being led down to the field. A woman with a strident voice was teaching a small group of teenagers in the outdoor school. Drew glanced around. As usual, he was the only bloke on the yard, unless you counted one of the dads, sitting in his car, staring intently at the screen of his mobile phone.

Siegfried plodded out happily when Drew led him to the field, not a hint of yesterday's excitement. Drew watched him amble off to graze, turned and went back to the yard. He had just started mucking out when Gemma appeared.

'You know I could do that for you,' she said.

'Uh-huh. But you'd add it to my bill, and I can't afford it.'

'That bad, huh?'

'Yup.' Drew stopped what he was doing, and leant on the handle of the shavings fork. 'I know you said you'd put the feelers out to see if anyone was interested in Siegfried, but I think it's time to formally advertise.'

Gemma nodded slowly. 'OK, if you're sure. Want me to put the ad together?'

'Please.' Drew grinned. 'Otherwise it'll say something like "Big brown horse, eats like...a horse. Good for...riding" or something equally rubbish.'

Gemma rolled her eyes. 'Yeah, better leave it to me!'

'Anyway, did you have a nice horseless evening?' asked Drew.

'Oh, don't!'

'That good?'

Gemma shook her head. 'I was meeting someone I've got to know online. It's ridiculous - on email and on the phone, he's great. Funny, interesting, intelligent. But face to face - well, we just looked at each other and there was nothing there, you know? I mean, it was an OK evening, nice food and everything, but I couldn't help thinking this is my first night off for weeks and I'm wasting it - I could be out with the girls having a proper laugh!'

'Bummer.'

Gemma made a face. 'Sorry, I shouldn't be burdening you with my crappy love life.'

Drew aimed the fork at the next pile of dung. 'It's fine - I'm enjoying the stories vicariously. Though the thought of being ready for all that scares me to death.'

'Bless you,' said Gemma. 'You'll be hard pushed to find another Caroline.'

Drew blew out his cheeks. 'I don't want to. She was one in a million.'

'For an old nag, you look the business, don't you?'

Siegfried nosed the advert pinned to the front of his stable door. There was a colour picture of the big bay flying over a spread fence of coloured poles, Caroline crouched low over his withers, her slender frame dwarfed by her mount.

'Don't dribble on it,' said Drew, pushing him back, and pulling open the stable door. 'In you go.'

Siegfried went straight to his haynet.

'Now remember, I need you to be on your best behaviour when anyone comes to see you, OK?'

'And I'm sure he understands everything you say!' said Gemma, coming out of the next-door stable and fastening the bolt.

'Of course he does - he just chooses to ignore it,' said Drew. 'Thanks for doing the ad. Looks great.'

'No probs - it's on the website, and posted up at a few places locally.' Gemma glanced at Siegfried over the stable door. 'You know, it wouldn't hurt for you to keep him ticking over while you're waiting for a buyer. Nothing major, just sit on him and plod around the school a bit. Just to remind him what it's all about. He's an old hand, but they go a bit feral if you don't keep them in regular work. I could get one of the girls to pop him on the lunge once in a while, but we've not got the staff to work him properly. You do ride, don't you?'

Drew pondered the question. Yes, he'd ridden a bit as a kid. He knew how to get on the bloody things, and he could start and stop and steer. And he'd pretty much mastered the rising trot on Siegfried. A couple of years ago in the spring time, he and Caroline had started hacking out together, Caroline borrowing another horse, and Drew riding Siegfried, and they'd pottered around the local farm tracks in the evenings, while the sun slanted across the sky, and freshly minted leaves bobbed on the trees over their heads. But then Drew had got involved in a new project at work which meant he was home later in the evenings. After that, the winter had come and it was dark after work, and by the time the lighter nights had arrived, Caroline hadn't been up to riding anymore. The last time she tried to ride in the school, Drew remembered having to half lift her off Siegfried's back and carry her to the car, she was so exhausted. Siegfried had stood like a rock, as if knowing something was wrong.

'Yeah, OK,' said Drew, unwillingly. 'I'll give it a go.'

'You could walk him round the school for a few minutes now, if you want. It's dark, but I can put the floodlights on. No-one else has booked it.'

Drew thought of simply going home, stopping at the chippy on the way, sticking a film on, and supervising the sofa for the evening.

'Yeah, alright. Just a few minutes then. Remind me which is his tack.'

The floodlights cast eerie shadows at the edges of the arena, but it was fine riding in the middle, around the poles left over from the lesson. It was a bit uncomfortable in jeans, and he could hear Caroline's voice scolding him for riding in wellies, but hey, he'd not planned this. The hat he'd borrowed fitted fine, but he couldn't help wondering how many other sweaty heads had worn it. Siegfried's long neck bobbed in front of him, his dark mane falling in a tangled mess on the right. Caroline would have had something to say about that - leaving him looking such a state - but there was no-one to see.

It felt surprisingly good being back in the saddle. He'd not actively missed it, but feeling the rhythm of Siegfried's long stride beneath him was calming. The reins were clumsy in his hands, but when he turned Siegfried across the school, the horse responded readily enough.

After a couple of minutes Drew said, 'Hey mate, fancy a trot?' Siegfried's ears flicked towards him at the sound of his voice. 'Trot on then.' Drew gave him a nudge with his heels, and Siegfried, slightly surprised, lumbered into a trot for a few strides, and then walked again, as if saying 'Are you sure?' Drew used his legs again, a bit more firmly, and this time Siegfried strode out, and kept the rhythm. They did a full lap of the arena before Drew pulled up and gave Siegfried a pat. 'Well done, mate! Let's have a breather and then have a go the other way.'

This time they did a lap, and trotted over a pole lying on the floor. Siegfried put in just a little bit more effort than was required, so it felt like a half jump.

'You fancy that, do you, mate?' asked Drew. 'What about the proper little jump?'

There were two coloured poles set up in a tiny cross on the right of the arena. Drew put Siegfried into trot again, and pointed him at the jump. He wasn't really sure what you were meant to do, but he'd watched Caroline jump hundreds of times. She always leant forwards as she went over the fence. She said it was important not to yank the horse in the mouth when you were trying to keep your balance. Drew left his reins loose and grabbed a bit of the tangled mane. Just before the fence, Siegfried's gait change - they were cantering! Another stride, and pop, they were over the fence, two more canter strides and then Siegfried went back to trot and then walk.

'Hey! Well done, mate!' said Drew, patting him enthusiastically on the neck. 'That was brilliant! There's a good lad.' A grin spread across Drew's face. 'Good chap! I think that's enough for tonight. We'll have a last walk round and then you can go back and have some grub, eh?'

The grin wouldn't go away. How silly. It was just a tiddly jump. Hardly the Grand National! Why was he feeling so pleased with himself? But he found that he was whistling while he untacked Siegfried and threw on his rug. And even though his leg muscles were protesting as he hefted the saddle to the tack room, there was an extra spring in his step which he'd not felt for months.

The loft was rammed. He'd come up to look for his riding stuff. Caroline had bought him some jodhs a couple of years ago when he'd briefly taken up riding with her, and there was definitely a proper hat, but he had no idea where to start looking.

'How did we end up with all this stuff?' he said aloud, his eyes scanning the boxes and bags of stuff, stuff and more stuff.

They'd bought the house a couple of years after they'd first got together. They'd meant to do it up, stick it back on the market and move on, but they'd become attached to the place and the more they did to improve it, the more comfortable they got, and slowly the idea of selling it on had fallen by the wayside. The loft was testament to the roots they'd put down, and to the junk they'd filled their lives with.

Drew pulled a random box towards him. Old videos. Their last video recorder was long gone, so why were they keeping them? Why was *he* keeping them?

He'd seen something on social media the previous week. *'All that clutter used to be money. All that money used to be time.'*

Time! That's what he so desperately wished they'd had more of. More time together. And if he'd not been working all hours before she'd got sick, maybe...

He threw the box of videos out of the loft hatch, and listened to them fall with a crash onto the landing and scatter down the stairs.

There were tears rolling down his cheeks as he pulled the next box towards him.

It took him several weekends to fully clear the loft. To begin with he wanted to simply throw it all away, but the practical difficulties stopped him, and besides, he could hear Caroline's voice in his head muttering about landfill. Some of the stuff was tat, granted. But not all. He advertised some for free collection. Some could go to charity, the rest he'd sell. He started being methodical, organising all the stuff into piles in the spare room. The ladies at the charity shops in town started to recognise him.

He found his breeches, some old boots, and his hat (packed properly in its original box) in his second night of rummaging. He started making an effort to ride a few evenings a week, in the weird glow of the flood lights. Most of the time he simply rode around the edges, or rode circles like he remembered Caroline doing. When he felt brave, and when Siegfried seemed up for it, he tried a few canters, but their steering tended to get a bit messy at speed. Very occasionally, someone would leave a jump up, and they'd pop over it. Those were the rides which left Drew buzzing.

One Sunday, Janet, a spritely woman in her seventies, asked if he'd like to potter out with her for a 'safe-as-houses' ride around the block. And so, he found himself on Siegfried beside Janet and her cob Ollie, out in the fresh air on a sharp but sunny morning, when normally he'd have been at home, slobbing in front of the TV. Riding back into the yard, he couldn't believe the feeling of achievement.

While he was untacking Siegfried, Gemma popped her head over the stable door and said, 'I've had a call from some people interested in your horse.'

Drew rested the saddle over the door; all the bubbles inside him immediately went flat.

'What did they say?'

'They'd like to come and see him this afternoon, if that's convenient. They're from somewhere down south, happened to be in the area looking at another horse, and just saw the advert by chance.'

'They're coming today?' Drew glanced at Siegfried. It seemed suddenly painful that the bay horse was so oblivious. This afternoon someone else might agree to buy him - to take him away from the place which had been his home for several years. That morning's ride might have been the last time he and Siegfried would potter around the lanes together. The thought brought a lump to Drew's throat. Ridiculous. This was what he wanted. To be shot of the responsibility and the expense.

'It's alright - I'll get one of the girls to give them a demo - you won't have to get back on!' Gemma eyes were full of amusement.

'It's not that...' Drew glanced at Siegfried again. 'It's...' He stopped. 'It's going to sound silly, but I don't think I can do it.'

'Do what?'

'Sell him.' He looked helplessly at Gemma. 'These past few weeks...they've been the best I've felt since Caroline died. And it's Siegfried who's been the reason for that.

Having him to look after has made me more disciplined about leaving work on time. In the mornings, I don't lie in bed feeling sorry for myself, I get up and come here, and just walking him down to the field, and mucking out his bed, and getting his hay ready - it's bizarrely therapeutic. I feel like I'm connected to Caroline through him, but not thinking about her in a maudlin way.' He paused. 'Does all that sound really soft?'

Gemma shook her head. 'Not in the slightest. But what about your cash flow problems?'

'I've made a lot of changes over the last few weeks,' said Drew, draping Siegfried's bridle across his saddle. 'Cancelled subscriptions to things I really didn't need. Sold some stuff. Got my spending under control. I'm not flush, but I can manage.'

'Want me to go and tell them sorry, he's no longer for sale?'

Drew came out of the stable, pulled the bolt across, and ripped the advert off the door. 'Yeah, sorry to mess you about - but if you could, that would be great.'

Gemma grinned. 'I was hoping you'd say that!' She squeezed his arm, turned and headed back to the office.

Drew let out the breath he'd been holding. 'Wanna stick with me, buddy?' he said to Siegfried.

The horse came forward at the sound of his voice, stuck his head over the door, and butted Drew's hand gently. Drew ran his fingers over the familiar white blaze and said, 'You can't sell a mate, can you?'

He lifted Siegfried's tack from the door and started to walk to the car. He imagined Caroline watching him taking his tack home to clean! He remembered all the times he'd grumbled at her for cleaning her tack on the floor in the lounge. And for the first time the memory made him smile.

BOX REST

The alarm on my phone trills under my pillow, dragging me out of my dreams and into the pale reality. I shake it into silence, and out of habit go to swing my legs out of the bed, to head to the yard, check the horses and get on with the day.

The pain brings me up short. It's so vivid it takes my breath away and I hang, half in, half out of bed, gasping and waiting for it to subside. The pain is everything. The room disappears. Light and temperature are as nothing. The shock of it sings in my ears. Breathe. Breathe. It will go.

Slowly, my limbs become mine again; I notice my bodyweight on the bed, the sharpness of the air, the thin sliver of grey from the crack in the curtains. Gently, carefully, I lay back on the pillows. Puff out a breath. Relax.

Why on earth did I enable the alarm? Because I am home? But I'm not in my own room. I'm in a narrow single bed in what was advertised as the dining room when I bought the house. It's a gloomy, pokey room and since I'm not one for dinner parties or dining, up to now it's just been a space for storing my tack and spare rugs. Usually I have a small desk in here so that I can work in the evenings. I'm not a hundred percent sure where the single bed has come from.

I hear a clunk from the kitchen, and the kettle goes on. Immediately my skin prickles. For the last nine years I have lived alone, so having someone else in my house is enough to make my nerves jangle. Knowing that it's my mother doesn't make it any better. From the age of 18 I've been taking care of myself. I've no wish for this to change. But she used my being in hospital to inveigle her way back into my life; they wouldn't let me out without ensuring I had someone at home to look after me. The NHS staff were not to know that the idea of my mother being the person to do that is laughable.

I hear her step in the hall and consider pretending to be still asleep. No, she probably heard my abortive attempt to get up. And besides, I'm not one for backing away from a confrontation. Yes, there's the pathetic, timid knock on the door - and in she comes, eyes steadfastly on the tray in her hand, not meeting mine.

'Morning sweetheart,' she says, her soft, singsong voice almost a whisper. It's the voice she always used with my stepfather on the bad days. 'I've brought you some tea and your tablets.'

Her hair looks particularly awful today. Her customary dye has grown out and she looks like a little old lady well before her time. The silver grey locks curl in random wisps. She needs a decent hairdresser to create some kind of order from the chaos. It's not like she can't afford it.

She tries to set down the tray on the cupboard which has been pushed into place as a bedside table, but there's not enough space next to the lamp, and she hesitates. I know what she's thinking. There's no coaster.

I take the mug from the tray and put it straight down on the cupboard top. It's only the flat-pack kind from the internet. I don't care about heat damage.

'Oh,' she makes a little gasp, 'are you sure?'

I can't answer. Reaching across has made me shift my weight slightly to the right. I bite my lip to prevent a grunt of pain.

She leaves the tablets in a little saucer next to my mug and stands the tray up against the wall.

'And how did you sleep?' she ventures.

'Fine,' I lie, adding, 'I need the toilet.'

I throw the covers off my legs and try not to look at the livid bruising. Fortunately the aftermath of the surgery is mostly hidden by my nightshirt.

My mother passes me the crutches and I do my best to ignore the 'oooh oooh' noises she makes as she watches me heave myself up, ineffectually putting her hands on my back. She moves to open the door wide, and hovers while I inch my way across the carpet.

The humiliation of needing my mother to help me in the narrow downstairs toilet makes me sweaty with shame. She leaves me some privacy, but I still need her help afterward to get back to bed. The whole ordeal takes about 20 times longer than it ought, and I'm eaten up with frustration by the time I am back, propped up on the pillows.

My mother props one crutch up by the cupboard and the other against the bottom of the bed. This is thoughtful and useful but my thanks come out like a dismissal.

I glance at the window. 'Oh, could you open the curtains?'

'Of course!' She leaps to perform the task, making a show of pushing them back as far as they will go. Greyish light pours into the room. I see the top of a bush being buffeted by the wind, grubby clouds scudding by in the distance. 'There,' she says. 'Not a very nice day, I'm afraid.'

I grunt. 'Makes no odds to me, stuck here.'

'No, you poor thing.' She gazes at me, eyes filled with concern.

'I'll live!' I answer, batting her sympathy away with irritation.

She tries again. 'What would you like for breakfast?'

'Nothing. I'm fine.'

'If you're sure? You maybe ought -'

'Really, I'm fine,' I say a little more sharply.

'OK,' she says. 'I'm going to pop to the shops in a bit. Is there anything you need?'

I shake my head.

'Can I get you a magazine or something?'

'No, thanks.' I glance across the room. At the other end of the cupboard is a pile of paperwork and a laptop bag. 'Can you just pass me my stuff?'

'Oh, Laura,' she sighs. 'You can't want to work - you're signed off. They know all about the accident. You should be concentrating on getting better.'

I don't respond. I stare at the pile of stuff. After a few seconds she goes to fetch it, sliding it gently onto the bed beside me. I unzip the laptop bag and passing her the end of the charger cable say, 'Can you plug me in.'

It takes her an age to find the power socket, while I fight down the urge to swipe the plug out of her hand and do it myself. But of course, I can't lean down that far. Finally the power light glows on my laptop, and I start it up.

'Thanks,' I say, glancing up at her. 'I'll be OK now.'

'If you're sure?' she says doubtfully. 'Please don't do too much, will you?'

'It'll take my mind off the pain,' I mutter.

'Yes, I suppose.' She gives me a tight smile. 'OK then, if there's nothing else I can get for you - ?'

I shake my head, my eyes on the laptop screen, typing in my password.

She hovers for a moment more then slips out quietly, shutting the door so gently I don't even hear the latch click.

My laptop dings and the screen is filled with my background image - a photograph of me and Dexter soaring over a huge tiger trap at an event two years previously. Dexter has cleared it by miles and I have a huge grin plastered across my face. I remember the supreme confidence I'd felt at that moment; that Dexter could jump the moon.

The thought springs into my mind: will I ever feel like that again?

And then another thought: what if I'd been riding Dexter three weeks ago instead of Scout. Would I be having a normal day in the office right now, not this pointless existence trapped in bed?

But I dismiss this immediately. It's fruitless conjecture, not least because Dexter's competition days are over.

I pull my phone out from under my pillow, flick to my contacts, and select the mobile number for Rachel, the owner of the livery yard where my two horses are kept. It goes straight to answerphone, and I leave a short message, before deciding to try the office phone. This rings out for an age before finally a woman's breathless voice answers.

'Hi Rach, it's Laura. Just wanted to check on the boys.'

'Oh my God, so good to hear from you!' Rachel's voice goes up a few octaves.

'Tried your mobile, but - '

Rachel makes a groaning noise. 'I've dropped it somewhere. God knows where. I'm going crazy without it!' She laughs, and says, 'Anyway, how are you doing?'

'Been better!' I respond ruefully.

'God, you gave us a fright!' she goes on. 'How are you feeling after the op? How's the pain?'

I glance at the tablets in the little saucer. 'OK.' I slide open the cupboard drawer and tip the tablets in with the others. The little round ones don't seem to do anything, and the oval ones make me feel sick and spaced out so I've stopped taking them.

'How's Scout?' I ask. 'I know the vet was happy with him after the fall, but I'm concerned there might be something which doesn't show up straightaway.'

'He's absolutely fine,' said Rachel. 'We've done exactly

as you asked. He's out on his own during the day where we can keep an eye on him - in the paddock next to the show jump field. And he's in at night, with an extra thick bed. I've checked his legs morning and evening. Claire has been riding him six days a week - and she's looked out for problems with his back. He's as sound as a pound.'

'And what sort of things has she done with him?' I ask quickly.

'Just like you said, did nothing but walk him out round the lanes for the first week. Since then she's mixed it up with flatwork, schooling over grids, and a hack out round the fields with a bit of canter work. No soundness issues at all. And she says he's been an absolute star - for a youngster, she can't believe how good he is.'

My heart tumbles over, a weird mix of pleasure at hearing so many positives, and jealousy because it's Claire, not me, who is getting to do all this.

'That's such a relief,' I tell her. 'And what about Dexter?'

'Well now,' says Rachel with a laugh, 'he's turned into an old grump. He makes faces at whoever goes into his box. The other day when I popped him on the horse walker he actually cow kicked at me.'

'Wonder what's up with him,' I muse. 'He's never been like that.'

'He's missing you of course!' says Rachel.

I laugh ruefully. 'He's a horse. He doesn't care who looks after him, so long as they remember the grub!'

Rachel makes a noise of protest as I knew she would. To Rach, all the horses in her care are individual personalities in their own right - which is one of the reasons her yard is so well run. For me, it's different. If I can't get Dexter sound again, I may have to claim on the insurance for loss of use. But that still won't get around the uncomfortable decision whether or not to have him put down. Keeping a pet horse on livery is an expensive business.

'Well, give him a pat for me,' I tell her. 'Wish I was able to get there.'

Rachel sighs. 'I know you'll want to be here as soon as, but you've got to look after yourself first.'

'Yeah, yeah - I've got physio tomorrow. Once I have the exercises to practise, I'll be back on my feet - don't you worry.'

Rach makes a noise of disbelief. 'Look, your boys are doing fine. Make sure you give yourself the same care you would them, hey?'

I thank her and ring off. She's right, if it was one of them, I would be making sure they had all the right medication and care. I look in the drawer again, take out one of the little round pills, and swallow it with a gulp of tea. I still can't face those nasty oval ones.

I log into my work email. There are only a handful of messages - all are of the 'all staff' variety. Someone (not me) has set up an 'out of office' reply that indicates the two people who should be contacted in my absence. Neither of the suggestions fills me with confidence. I'll have a mountain of things to sort out when I get back. And how can I do that if email is being diverted to other people's mailboxes? A wave of frustration overwhelms me once again.

I click out of the email, and open up my training plan spreadsheet. I have a separate tab for each horse, and the schedule is mapped out with lessons, events, and training programmes all built in. I glance over the original schedule for Scout this week, then the events we had lined up over the forthcoming months, and feel sick with disappointment. I need to cancel all the event entries. I need to re-work Scout's training plan. I need to.... My eyes are heavy. I close them for just a second.

When I wake, the laptop has slid off my lap and onto the bed. The screensaver has come on - a slideshow of photographs. I never usually see this - my laptop is never idle for long enough - but there are hundreds of photos stored in some cloud or other, and now the screen saver program has plucked them at random from its virtual memory, and presented them on screen. Holiday snaps from places long since forgotten, Dexter peering from the horsebox on the day he arrived as a three year old, a random shot from someone's wedding. Then there is a photo of me aged about 15 sitting on a smart bay. My face is impassive. Both pony and I are impeccably turned out. My long black boots are polished to perfection. His plaits are tiny and admirably uniform, and there is a red rosette pinned to his bridle. I don't remember the pony's name.

The image changes. A couple of arty shots - a sunset, a seascape. Then the lorry when I first picked it up three years ago - it had taken me years to save up for that! I smile, and am just about to touch the mouse pad to flick off this nostalgia trip when Frog appears.

My heart clenches as it does every time I see this photo. Dear Frog! The little dun gelding, with the huge brown eyes and tufty forelock. His jumping name was Frogeye Sprite. His door plaque said 'Sprite', and so did his feed bucket, but to me he was Frog, and how I had loved him. Dear, dear Frog. In the photo, I have my arms around his neck and I'm grinning and grinning like a mad thing. I'm about 10 years old. I look so happy.

The front door squeaks and clunks. My mother is back from shopping. I close the lid of the laptop, push it out of the way, and reach carefully for the crutch to my left. With or without the physiotherapist, my rehabilitation starts right now.

I try to be quiet but, after a few minutes, inevitably she comes in with another mug of tea.

'Laura! What are you doing?'

'Practising walking.'

'But you should be resting.'

'I've had enough rest. I've been asleep for ages.'

'At least let me help,' she says, coming into the room,

and setting the tea down on the side table.

'I don't need any help.'

'Please?'

I round on her. Standing there with that pathetic expression on her face, I want to shake her. Suddenly I know how my stepfather felt.

'Just let me be.'

I carry on, slowly, painfully, focusing on the pattern in the carpet, trying not to think about Frog and everything else from back then.

Behind me, I hear the door shut gently. I feel a stab of remorse. But it's too late. Too late for her to want to protect me.

I walk (it's not walking, not really, just shuffling) until the pain is so intense there are tears rolling down my cheeks. Now I know how poor old Dexter felt immediately after his tendon injury. He's better now, and when he's walking around the yard he almost looks sound, but I know it's still not properly fixed. I won't let them turn him out in a paddock. The poor chap is confined to his box, the horse walker and the occasional half hour grazing in hand. It's not surprising he's turning into an old grump.

It takes a few minutes, and a lot of puffing, before I'm back in bed. I feel a bit sick. And my heart is heavy.

I pull the laptop towards me. When I open it up, my face is reflected in the black screen.

Am I turning into him?

I stare at the reflection, searching for traces of him in my features. Impossible. He wasn't my father after all.

When she first met him, I'd have been about eight. She was very careful to introduce him to me gradually. He didn't come to the house, those first few times - we went out to meet him, and we'd do something low key; go to the park and feed the ducks, go for an ice-cream. Once we hired a little rowing boat and bobbed about on the water. I remember he let me row for a bit, and I felt so grown-up to be trusted with this - and he was patient, explaining how to hold the oars, how to make the boat turn one way or the other. And my mum's eyes shone because we were getting on so well.

My reflection gazes back at me. People often assumed he was my dad, and we neither of us ever bothered to correct them. I suppose it was plausible. My eyes are blue like his were, and I have the same kind of jaw line. But my hair is definitely from my mother. It looks a state now, just like hers, but at least I've got an excuse.

I boot up the laptop and this time I actively search through the memory bank of photographs. While I search, I find myself thinking about stuff I have tried hard to bury for a long time.

I find a picture of the three of us having a meal, sitting around a wooden picnic bench in a pub beer garden somewhere. It's my 11th birthday, I'm wearing a party frock way too dressy for the pub. I have a ridiculously large knickerbocker glory, and am grinning at the camera.

I remember how I felt at that moment. Something like triumph. I'd just had a glowing school report, my room was tidy, I'd won my jumping class on Frog at the riding club that morning. I hadn't outgrown anything recently or accidentally walked into a room when my stepfather had an important visitor, so I was a good girl. Nothing could spoil my birthday evening.

In the photograph, my mother and stepfather sit across from me. My stepfather (who had insisted on the knickerbocker glory) is smiling at me. My mother has her head slightly turned towards him. Her expression is a curious mix; there is a smile on her lips, but her eyes betray concern. By now, she knows how fragile these moments can be.

I remember how the rest of that evening turned out. I was sick in the car on the way home - my stepfather always drove so fast, the lanes were winding, and he wouldn't stop when I asked. When we got home, he marched me through the house, still covered in my own vomit, and stood me in the kitchen garden. He made me take off the gorgeous party frock, and despite my mother saying it was fine, that she would put it in the wash, he threw it on the bonfire pile and set fire to the lot. I watched the fabric melt and blacken, the little plastic diamonds sewn into the material liquefying before my eyes, and then the whole thing went up in flames. He told me to stop crying, put some clothes on and clean the rest of the vomit out of his car.

I was sick in the front flower border twice more while I was cleaning the upholstery of his fancy BMW. I cried the whole time, covered in snot and tears and vomit, and at one point, I glanced up at the house, and there was my mother watching from the bedroom window.

Yeah, memorable birthday that.

The following day is my first physio session as an outpatient. My mother drives me to the hospital. She drives in the same way she does everything else; anxiously, nervously, hesitantly, overthinking every decision. I find it best not to look through the windscreen, but instead to stare out of the passenger window fixedly, doing my best to ignore her small exclamations of breathless concern as another car comes slightly too close, or cuts her up as the lanes merge.

We finally make it to the hospital, negotiate the difficulty of my being dropped off outside the appropriate entrance, and it's not long before we're in the bland pastel coloured waiting room. I choose to stay standing, and am relieved when the physio - a guy in his late thirties - calls my name.

We follow him into the small, equally bland physio room.

'This is my mother,' I say, inclining my head towards her.

'Hello Laura's mother,' says the physio, slightly amused.

'Oh, *Jackie*!' says my mother, and gives a little giggle, the kind I've not heard for years.

'Hello, Jackie.' He starts to flick through my notes, looks up, fixes me with a hard stare and says, 'Came off a horse, eh?'

I make a face. 'Technically, we both fell.'

He makes a single considered nod at this amendment to the facts. 'Horse alright?'

'Yes,' I reply, surprised. 'He's fine.' None of the other medical staff has asked this question.

'Good. Don't suppose you've come to your senses and decided to take up stamp collecting instead?'

I grin, and look at him properly for the first time. He has sandy coloured hair which is a bit messy, and greyish blue eyes which are lively with amusement.

'No. But I'm guessing I'm not going to be back in the saddle any time soon.'

'Nope. Don't think so.' He looks up, meets my gaze steadily. 'But what we do here will help determine how quickly that might become a possibility.'

'Might?' I feel something tumble down inside me. It had occurred to me that realistically I might not be able to compete to the same level again. I had not considered that I might not be able to ride at all.

The physio makes a thoughtful face. 'I'm sure the doctors have already spoken to you about recovery from these kinds of injuries, and in any case, whether you choose to get back on a horse again is largely up to you. I just want you to be aware that this was a serious fall, and though my colleagues have done an amazing job pinning you back together, there is likely to be some long term stiffness, coupled with muscle and tissue damage, and compromised movement of the hip joint.'

I nod.

'I'll warn you now, a lot of this is going to be uncomfortable, or worse. I will, of course, be guided by how far you feel you can push yourself. But what I'm trying to say is that the extent to which you get full mobility back is determined for the large part by you. Hope you don't think I'm being harsh - I'm just trying to give you the facts. OK?'

I clench my jaw and nod again.

'OK then. We'll do some exercises here today, and I'll give you some more straightforward ones to do at home before your next session. Obviously, if you can do those regularly, you'll make better progress than if you don't.'

'Oh, she'll do them,' says my mother. 'She's very driven.'

He looks at me with interest, then says, 'Good.'

Turns out he wasn't kidding.

By the time we get home, I feel as if I've endured some kind of medieval torture. I take the tablets my mother fetches for me, and when she's gone, I fish out an extra one of the oval shaped ones from my drawer and take that as well. Then I sleep for about five hours.

I'm woken by my phone pinging. It's a message from Claire. With a bit of puffing, I manage to get myself propped up on some pillows, and click on the message. It's a video of Scout being loose-schooled. His stride is easy and athletic, his natural balance obvious on the turns, and he pops the grid of three jumps in text-book fashion. I send her a thumbs up and smiley face. I'm so pleased that he seems none the worse for his ordeal. Then a thought strikes me.

I send a second message to Claire to ask her if she would like me to keep him entered in his next event - with her riding instead of me.

I get an answer straightaway. There's lots of exclamation marks and a grinning emoji. So that's a yes then.

Cradling the phone, I lie back on the pillows. What will it be like to be an owner, not a rider, watching someone else compete on my horse?

Beneath all the uncertainty and resentment, there is something else. Claire is a talented rider, but earns a pittance from her part time work at Rachel's yard, and has to supplement her income with bar work in the evenings. I know she can't afford a quality horse like Scout, so having the opportunity to compete on him will mean the world to her. I'm not very good at making friends, so it's a novelty doing something nice for someone else. It's a good feeling, a warm feeling.

My mother puts her head round the door to check on me, and once again we go through the palaver of getting me to the bathroom and back. Then she brings in a tray.

'Thought you'd be hungry,' she says.

There's a plate of neat little sandwiches - triangles with the crusts cut off! And a few grapes, some small squares of what is probably chocolate brownie, and a tall glass of sparking water.

'Thank you!' I say. And I find I mean it.

She turns to leave and I say, 'Stay and have a piece of brownie?' I motion at the chair at the bottom of the bed for her to sit.

She pauses, and the pause makes me realise how vile I've been to her since she arrived.

'No brownie for me - it sticks here,' she taps her hips ruefully. 'But if you want some company...?'

She sits down very gently, always careful. So careful in everything she does.

'This is all spot on,' I tell her, between mouthfuls. 'I've not really fancied anything for days, but this is perfect.'

She gives a small smile, but does not meet my gaze.

'It's frustrating for you, isn't it?' she says. 'Being stuck here. Not being able to get on.'

'Yup.' I sigh. 'And it's all my fault. Not Scout's. He was doing his best.'

Mum gives a tiny shake of her head and a tight smile. 'You always said that when you were a kid. Whenever you came off, always blamed yourself - never the pony.'

'Yeah, well, it was safer that way.' I purse my lips.

She allows a few moments to pass, the silence thick in the air between us. Then she asks, 'Can you remember it all now, clearly, the accident?'

'Yes.'

I picture the scene I've run through so many times in my head. We're three quarters of the way around the cross country course, we've got through all the bogey fences I was worried about and we're on the long canter down to an innocuous looking log pile. The path is flanked on either side by trees, and their branches meet above us, casting dancing shadows on the grass beneath Scout's hooves. When we come out of the trees, the sunlight is startling, and the fence seems suddenly too close so that, even though Scout is on the perfect stride and is travelling easily beneath me, I feel the need to take a pull on the reins. And that's what does it; we momentarily lose impulsion, and it is enough so that Scout has to put in an extra stride. He does his best, takes a tremendous leap, but suddenly we are spinning.

I've fallen lots of times in my life, and always got up. But this time Scout rolls over me, and as I watch him clamber to his feet, I realise that I am unable to follow suit. I am broken. And as the First Aid guys run towards me, I feel the first stab of genuine fear.

'It was my fault,' I repeat. 'I was tired. I'd been working late every night that week. But we'd been training so hard, and he was going so well, I didn't want to scratch. He was going beautifully. We'd have been placed, I'm sure.'

Mum says, 'You drive yourself too hard.'

I glance at her. 'And I wonder why that is.'

She looks down at her hands, twists her wedding ring, and sighs.

I eat my brownie.

It's not until the following day that I study the two pieces of A4 paper given to me by the physio. They contain diagrams and instructions for six different exercises I should do to improve my muscle tone and movement - he ran through them at the end of the session, but I have to admit, by then I was in so much pain I was hardly listening. At the bottom of the final page there is a hand written note. 'Remember, much like with horses, steady walking is often the best way back to fitness after an injury - so try to mix these with some walking when possible. S.'

S. For some reason, I think his name is Simon, but I don't know why I think this. He didn't introduce himself by name, and he wasn't wearing a name badge.

I stretch my hand out carefully to the top of the cupboard, and my fingertips find the letter which confirmed the appointment.

Physiotherapist: Simon Creed.

Hmm. So, Simon seems to know something about horses. I pick up my phone, open the Facebook app, and search his name. There are several Simon Creeds. I squint at the profile pictures. None of them look like him, but one is of a horse's head. The horse is wearing giant yellow sunglasses. I click on the profile.

Simon's profile page opens. His cover photo is a sunset over a field, and a horse in almost silhouette grazing slightly to the left of centre. It's a great photo - the oranges and pinks of the sky, the position of the horse, the way his tail is fanned out slightly as if by a gentle breeze.

I scroll down. It's definitely the right Simon Creed. He doesn't post much. Or more likely his privacy settings don't allow me to see what he posts. (Very sensible, given that presumably I'm not the only patient who has engaged in a little Facebook stalking.) He's been tagged by other people in a few photos from several months previously. In one, he and another guy are in a pub, pint glasses in hand, grinning. In another, he has his arm around the shoulder of a petite blonde girl - clearly not his sister from the way she is folded against him! The only other thing I can see is a post showing the fact of him updating his profile photo to the horse-in-sunglasses shot.

I close the app, push the covers off my legs and, with a grunt, start the process of getting out of bed. Time to get on with those exercises.

At lunch time, my mother brings me a cuppa, a cheese roll with a little side salad. This time she brings a mug of tea for herself too, and she sits again on the chair, sipping her tea while I eat.

'This is a nice little house,' she says, softly, thoughtfully.

I shrug. 'It suits me. And I can afford it on my own.'

'I'm thinking of moving to somewhere smaller.' She takes another sip of her tea.

The world tilts a little on its axis. Without wishing to, I picture the farmhouse as I last saw it, maybe fifteen years ago. A proper child's drawing of a house; warm red brick, with a beautiful arched front door in the centre and windows arranged symmetrically either side. An outbuilding off to the left which my stepfather had converted into a double garage. An L-shaped stable block at the back, behind the kitchen garden. A small paddock off to the right, and another field next to it which we rented. There were four bedrooms. My stepfather used one as a study. One was a guest room. Mine was at the back and overlooked the stable yard.

It was a dream house. A dream house about which I still have nightmares.

'Good,' I say. 'Silly for you to be knocking about in that old place by yourself.'

She looks down at her mug. 'Yes. And besides, I've realised since I've been here...being in a fresh place with no memories - well, it's like a weight being lifted.'

I glance at her, but she doesn't meet my eye.

'Anyway,' she goes on, 'I spoke to the solicitor when we were winding up Ray's estate.'

I flinch inwardly at the mention of his name. It's the first time I've heard her speak of his death.

'If I sell up, I won't need all the money to buy somewhere else just for me. I want you to have some of it.'

'I don't want it,' I say quickly.

'Laura, that's silly.'

'It's his money.'

'It was. But it's mine now. And I want you to have it.'

'I don't want it,' I repeat.

'That's just cutting off your nose to spite your face.' She is exasperated. '*I'm* giving it to you.'

'As if it makes everything OK?'

'No, of course not. But he wasn't a monster. He didn't abuse you or anything like that.'

'Not physically.'

She takes a breath, as if about to deliver a rehearsed speech. 'He had a very short temper and he was old fashioned - he liked things to be exactly how he wanted them. Yes, he was strict, and sometimes he overreacted to situations.'

A snort of derision escapes me. 'That's an understatement if ever there was! Overreacted? The man was a bully and a tyrant.'

'And he looked after us when I was at my lowest ebb.' My mother's voice is firm in a way I've never heard before. 'Remember, I was a single mum when he met me. We didn't have a penny. I was struggling to keep a roof over our heads, to keep us fed. I used to worry when you brought home a letter from school about some trip I couldn't afford, or...' She fishes for another example. 'I remember once you were doing cookery and you had to take in some ingredients - and I couldn't afford all the things on the list.' She chews her lip at the memory. 'I didn't want you to get bullied because I couldn't afford the right school uniform, or decent shoes. He took all that worry away. And look at all the things you had, thanks to him - all the ponies.'

I feel the breath catch in my throat. There have been plenty of times following the accident that I've felt irritated and frustrated at not being able to walk properly. But right this moment, I cannot bear to listen any more. I want to get up and run away. Instead I pick up my lunch plate and hurl it across the room. It hits the far wall and smashes into several pieces, scattering salad all over the floor.

My mother flinches, then turns to me, shaking her head slowly.

'I did my best, Laura. I always did my best. I'm sorry you think I failed.'

She gets to her feet, walks across the room with dignity, and goes out of the door, closing it softly behind her.

I stare at the bits of salad on the carpet and begin to cry.

*

I am 12. It's a Sunday in early summer. The following day I have to go on a week-long school trip. Much fuss has been made of this at home as this is a special residential trip for 'gifted' children in Science. It will be the first time I've stayed away on my own somewhere strange, without any of my other school friends. The other kids on the residential will come from other schools. I'm nervous - more nervous than I've let on. But worse than all this is the fact I won't see Frog for a whole five days. This feels like an eternity. He will be turned out, and mum will check on him, so I know he will be fine, but I'm not sure I will. I'm scared of waking up in the morning and not being able to lean out of my bedroom window to call to him. Of not being able to come home at the end of the day and run out to the paddock to see him.

So, on Sunday afternoon I take him for an extra-long ride and spend an extra-long time brushing him afterwards, and when I go to turn him out, I stand in the paddock with my arms around him for an age. My heart is heavy with dread.

And then suddenly I realise I am late for dinner.

Sunday dinner is sacrosanct in our household. And Sunday dinner before I leave for a week is particularly special. I give Frog a final kiss, close the field gate and run as fast as I can back to the house. I mutter prayers to any deity who cares to listen, willing time to somehow have moved into reverse, to erase those fateful minutes, but my heart is hammering as I slip in the back door. The clock on the kitchen wall confirms my doom. I'm 16 minutes late.

I take a breath. I'm shaking. I push open the dining room door. My mother and stepfather are both eating, their plates almost empty. Neither of them says a word. My dinner sits there, the gravy congealing. I slip into my seat, whisper 'Sorry I'm late,' and pick up my knife and fork.

Still no-one says anything. There is just the sound of cutlery scraping. And the grandfather clock in the background ticking off those fateful minutes.

*

Neither my mother nor I bring up our conversation again. After years of experience, we are both adept at this way of dealing with anything emotional. It took me an age to clear up all the bits of salad and broken plate. Since I couldn't reach down I had to improvise by dropping a piece of paper on the floor, and using a dressage whip which I found propped in the corner of the room to sort of flick the bits onto the paper. Obviously I couldn't pick up the paper afterwards, but I used the dressage whip to shove it over to the door so it was at least easy for my mother to collect, which she did later, without comment.

But despite the fact no further discussion has taken place, there is a subtle change. The conversation appears to have been cathartic for her. She carries herself differently; no longer seems so fawning or hesitant in her manners or movements. In turn, I find myself being not quite so much of a bitch. I feel stronger now. I join her for meals in the kitchen. I even sit in the lounge and watch telly with her in the evenings, though I have to sit very upright on a kitchen chair as the old sofa is too low and squashy.

By the time of my second physio session, the pain has started to ease off.

We've just arrived at the hospital, when I get another message from Claire. This time, it's a video of Dexter in his loose box. He's standing at the back of the box, with his ears back, and the most sulky expression I've ever seen on his face. Off camera I hear Rach saying, 'Are you ready?' And Claire's voice says 'Yup - go!' Then I hear my own voice. I realise Rach, who must have found her phone, is playing back my answerphone message from the previous week. At the sound of my voice, Dexter's head comes up, his ears go forward and he makes a little hurrumph noise. He comes to the front of his box, puts his head over the door and tries to work out where I am.

My heart turns over.

'Everything OK?' asks my mother, glancing at me.

I nod, but my eyes are misty. I show her the video.

She says, 'Oh bless him! She puts her hand gently on my leg, and says, 'You'll see him soon.'

It's the first time she's made such a gesture in years. I give her a watery smile.

Mum bumps into an old friend on our way to the Physio Dept. We pause for a moment, but both women obviously have a lot to catch up on, so I suggest that if they want to go for a coffee or something, I'll meet her afterwards.

Simon is pleased with my progress.

'You've been working hard,' he says, watching me demonstrate my speed-walking-with-crutches.

He examines my muscle development and range of movement. He's careful to tell me what he will do, and to check that I am OK with him touching me. I'm fine with that, though I feel fairly revolting personally. Since I can't make it up the stairs, I haven't been able to have a shower since I've been home. Strip washes using the hand basin in the downstairs loo are OK, but I'd do anything for a long soak in the bath and to be able to wash my greasy hair.

I watch his hands, deft and strong. His square nails are short and neat. When he crouches, the muscles in his thighs are taut under the blue uniform trousers. I realise I like being here, in this room with him. I like feeling that for the moment I can abdicate my responsibility. I have felt that weight for so long, I am exhausted by it.

He asks how I'm finding the exercises at home, and we go through some new ones. Occasionally he corrects something about my posture or technique. This time the whole process isn't quite so gruelling.

While I'm catching my breath and he's writing up his notes, he says, 'How's the horse?'

I show him the video of Scout.

'That's the one who fell?'

I nod.

'Looks as right as rain, doesn't he?' says Simon, tilting the phone a little so he can see the screen better.

'Yes, incredible really. If I don't go back to competing, I'll sell him on - he'd be wasted as a happy hacker.' Saying it out loud crystallises a thought I've only just acknowledged to myself.

The video comes to an end, and then the next one begins to play automatically.

'Who's this?'

'That's Dexter, my other horse - I've had him for ten years. Backed him and brought him on myself.'

Simon smiles as the video plays out. 'Wow - that's some bond you have with him.'

I nod. 'But weirdly I don't think I fully appreciated it before seeing that.'

Simon watches the video over again and says, 'He's a decent looking horse too.'

'He's on box rest.'

Simon grins at me. 'Just like you then?'

I make a face. 'Fortunately for him, it's not quite so serious - just a tendon injury we can't get right.'

'Did he do that while competing?'

'Yes - he tries too hard sometimes.'

Simon hands me my phone back. 'Just like you then?' he repeats softly.

Much to my embarrassment, I feel tears spring into my eyes. I rub a hand across them quickly, but Simon says, 'Sorry - now I've upset you.' He swipes a tissue box from the window sill and holds it out to me.

'No, it's not you!' I say quickly, taking a tissue, and grinning to show how foolish I am. 'I mean, you're absolutely right.' I take a deep breath. 'I've just been confronting some demons recently.'

'That's box rest for you,' says Simon. 'Too much time to think, hey?'

'Way too much - especially when you've been deliberately not-thinking for a long time.'

Simon fetches his own phone from a side table, opens his photo app and shows me a picture of a stunning chestnut, wearing a turquoise bridle.

'This is my boy.'

'Beautiful,' I say. 'Endurance horse, huh?'

'Was. We've given up the trophy hunting and the stop-watches. Now we just potter out for fun.'

'How come?'

'Some things changed in my life. Broke up with my partner - she was the one who was mad about endurance.'

The blonde girl from the Facebook photograph, I guess.

'Anyway, me and Foxy, we're both a hell of a lot happier. Not that I'm saying that would be right for everyone, but, you know, the world doesn't end just because you choose not to compete.'

'I know.' I sigh. 'But it might feel like it's ended if the choice isn't yours.'

He gives my arm a squeeze. 'With the progress you're

making, I don't think it'll come to that.'

I meet my mother in the foyer. She looks different; brighter somehow. I wonder if there's been lots of laughter in her conversation with her friend. In the car, we chat. She tells me about how long it's been since she's seen Kay, and how wonderful it was to talk about so many random things. I tell her about my appointment - the good progress I've made. About Simon showing me a photo of his horse. And then about him friending me on Facebook so he can send me details of an equine physio he knows who might be able to help with Dexter's lameness.

She glances at me and says 'You like him, don't you?'

I nod.

For a few moments, I savour this new idea; of liking Simon, of developing feelings for someone or something without risk or penalty.

I'm a grown up now. I can like whoever I want.

I feel a frisson of excitement.

Excitement and no dread.

I turn to my mum and say, 'Would you mind if we stopped off at the yard now? I really need to see Dexter.'

Rachel rushes to throw her arms around me, then pulls back at the last minute saying, 'Oh my God, is it OK to hug you?'

We embrace carefully, giggling, and she asks a million questions about my recovery, my exercises, how I feel.

We watch Scout grazing in the little paddock. I call his name, but he lifts his head only for a moment before returning to graze, and we laugh at his lack of interest. I tell Rachel the short-term and potential long-term plans I have for him. She nods and gives me another hug.

Then we go to the long barn, to the indoor stabling, and I creep up to Dexter's box. He's taking slow deliberate pulls from his haynet, and chewing thoughtfully. I say his name, and he pauses mid-chew, flicks an ear.

I get to within a few feet of the box and call him again. He leaves the hay, puts his head over the door and whickers softly. I make it all the way over to him. He sniffs the crutches with curiosity. I put my arms around his neck, lean against his cheek, breathe in the warm horsey smell of him. He rests his head on my shoulder.

I bloody love this horse. I can't believe I thought, even fleetingly, of having him put down. We will limp on together, the pair of us. I'll get Simon's mate out to fix Dexter, as Simon is helping to fix me.

I hug him so tight, he lifts his head a little as if to say, 'Steady on, mum!'

'Sorry, old boy,' I whisper. 'Just afraid to let you go.'

*

The week long residential trip has drawn to a close. It was actually quite fun. I've made friends with another girl and we've been inseparable for the week. I'm almost sad to leave. We swap addresses, hug, and promise to stay in touch (which, of course, doesn't happen). The previous Sunday dinner has almost become a distant memory, so much has happened in between. I assume it's been forgotten about. Only when I reach the car, and see the stony face of my stepfather do I realise that's far from the case. Part of the effectiveness of his punishments is that I can never be quite sure what form they will take or when they will be meted out.

My mum won't look at me. Her eyes are red and puffy. She's been crying. For a nanosecond, hope flares that possibly *she* has done something bad, something which has eclipsed my transgression, and perhaps that explains my stepfather's expression and his apparent refusal to talk to her either.

We travel home in silence. Neither of them asks about my week.

As soon as we get home, I jump out of the car ready to

run round to the stables, but my stepfather says I have to take my things up to my room first. I grab my bag and race upstairs, dump my stuff and glance out of the window. I can't see Frog. He must be in the very far corner of the field, sulking. I find the packet of mints I bought in the tuck shop at the residential centre, and I race downstairs, out of the back door, across the garden, and into the yard. Frog's stable door is shut up - the top door too, which is unusual. But I race onward to the field.

The gate is open. The field is empty.

For a second I think he's got out somehow. He's clever like that - he sometimes rubs his bum against the gate and pops the latch.

But the yard is too tidy, I see that now. I look in the tack room. His saddle and bridle and all his rugs are gone. Then I notice his name plate is missing from his stable door. When I lift the latch and peer inside, all the bedding has been cleaned out, his haynet and water bucket are gone. It's difficult to imagine there was ever a pony kept here.

I have discovered my punishment.

*

My progress walking to the water complex is slow but methodical. I am determined to manage on my own, despite the fact that mum is on one side and Simon on the other, ready to prop me up if I look like I'm faltering. Moments ago, the PA system announced that Claire and Scout had left the starting box and are now on their way down to the first fence.

Simon is carrying a shooting stick, and when we reach a suitable vantage point, he jams it in the ground, and lowers me onto the small seat. It's an ideal height meaning I won't get so stiff that I can't get back up again! He gives me a grin.

A horse and rider combination arrive at the water,

jump in, splash the three strides to the log, jump neatly, splash another two strides where upon the horse takes a dislike to something, makes a sudden leap sideways and catapults the rider into the water. There are cries of sympathy from the crowd. A steward manages to catch the horse. The rider, whose air-vest has gone off, struggles out of the water, panting and trying to zip herself free.

'Some advantages to not having to ride the course,' Simon observes.

I shake my head. 'Much worse watching, I can tell you!'

I feel sick. I estimate it'll be about four minutes before Claire and Scout tackle this fence.

Over the PA system, the commentator updates us on Claire's progress - and I hear my name mentioned as the horse's owner.

Simon gives me a gentle nudge.

I grin at him.

The commentator makes a cry of alarm, then there's the sound of him blowing out his cheeks. 'Bit sticky there over the Coffin, but she's through!'

'Bloody hell!' I gasp.

Claire comes into view, pops a corner, and without thinking, I grab Simon's hand. We watch Scout cantering up to the water complex. My heart is hammering against my chest. The muscles in my legs are tightening as, in my head, I'm squeezing Scout on, gathering him together.

He leaps over the rail into the water. His ears are pricked and he's focused on the log. Three perfect strides, he pops the log, another three perfect strides, and he hops out. He's made the whole thing look deceptively simple.

There is a smattering of applause. Simon squeezes my hand and we grin at each other as Scout canters smoothly away.

'Alright?' Simon asks.

I nod. 'Bit sweaty, but I think so!'

He puts his arm around my shoulders and gives me a gentle squeeze. I catch my mum's eye and exchange a smile. It's a genuine smile, and it means the world.

Much like Claire and Scout, I know we're not quite home and dry yet, but so far we're doing OK.

THE COMPANION PONY

Hilary gazed through the kitchen window at the paddock beyond the garden, and her heart turned over. A very small and very hairy bay pony stood by the fence, whinnying plaintively.

'Oh, Bramble!' Hilary fought the lump in her throat. It had been three weeks since they'd lost Jasper, Bramble's companion for the last nineteen years, and the remaining pony was clearly not enjoying his solitary existence. At first, Hilary had hoped that given time poor old Bramble would adjust, but as the days went by, and the normally happy, greedy pony continued to stand forlornly by the fence, whinnying for his lost friend, it was becoming obvious she would need to take action. A new companion was required.

Hilary was surprised to find the thought quite daunting. It was silly really. She'd had horses all her life. The children had all been through the horsey phase, so in the old days, there had been a succession of ponies coming and going. A string of faded rosettes hung along the wall, and the cabinet in the dining room was crammed with, admittedly now rather tarnished, trophies.

It didn't bear thinking about that, in some not-too-distant future, the kitchen window would overlook an empty paddock. Bramble himself was in his twenties now, and poor old Jasper had been even older. She had to face facts, she herself wasn't getting any younger. Ought she to find a new home for Bramble? Or…?

The 'or' brought tears to her eyes. No. Not yet. Not while he was still fit and healthy. Hilary took a carrot from the veg basket under the worktop, pushed open the back door, and picked her way across the grass to the fence. Bramble's ears pitched forward at the sight of her, and he let out another piercing whinny.

'You need a new friend, don't you little chap?' she said, scratching him behind the ears while he politely nibbled the carrot. There were grey hairs around his eyes and in the tufty hair of his bushy mane. But his coat was rich and shiny, and his eyes were bright. 'I promise, Bramble, you lovely old thing, to find you a new friend so you can live out your days in contented company.'

Bramble acknowledged her pledge by gently wiping some carrot-coloured slime on Hilary's jumper.

Hilary left him to finish his carrot with a thoughtful expression on his face, and went back into the empty house. She tried to push away the thought that it wasn't just Bramble who was feeling lonely. No, not lonely exactly. Unlike Bramble, she was quite content in her own company, most of the time. The loss of Jack, nine years earlier, had settled into a dull ache which only flared occasionally into full blown pain. The children, long flown, were great, popping in when they could. But it wasn't the same as having people around on a regular basis.

She stood in the kitchen chewing her lip. The air was still; the house holding its breath, waiting for some action from her. The clock in the hall ticked off the moments of her indecision.

In the paddock, Bramble let out another pitiful whinny. Her heart contracted.

'Come on, girl!' she told herself. She snatched up her

car keys and handbag, and headed out of the door.

The equine section of the local paper, which she read spread over the steering wheel of her car, yielded nothing of any interest, but the noticeboard in the feed merchants was awash with adverts. Hilary had taken down the details of three possible new friends for Bramble. The first had been an aged Shetland who'd initially sounded perfect, but turned out to be even older than the advert had suggested. When the owners had listed all his various ailments, Hilary decided it might be unwise to take him on. She had visions of huge vet bills, followed by lots more heartache, and a search for another replacement companion pony a few months down the line.

The next visit was to see five Welsh Mountain ponies needing re-homing. The wording had made it sound as though the place was a rescue centre, but it turned out to be a private ad. Hilary stood by the solid looking bungalow, and watched the ponies – all two year olds – careering around a small, muddy paddock, nipping and chasing each other. She made her decision in seconds. Poor old Bramble was too old for such antics.

'You'd have your pick, like.' The owner was a well-weathered man in his fifties, wearing aged boots and a waxed coat, the original colour of which was difficult to discern. He wouldn't quite meet Hilary's eye, but seemed to keep her in his peripheral vision. 'Or, I could let you have the lot for the price of four.'

Hilary had always had a weakness for Welsh Mountain ponies, with their pretty faces and huge eyes. How much fun she'd have had in her youth, bringing on five youngsters! But the thought now filled her with horror. It was obvious that taking even one home would be a grave mistake. She'd known that the moment she'd set eyes on them.

Apologising for wasting the gentleman's time, she made her way back to the car. On the passenger seat was her notepad. Just the final one to go. A child's riding pony seeking a quiet life; home more important than price. She called the number, and spoke to woman whose voice was laced with defeat. Yes, it would be convenient to see the pony now. Hilary typed the postcode into her SATNAV and set off.

The address was a neat brick house on an estate, where the door was answered by an anxious looking woman in her forties, and her pretty daughter, eyes red from crying.

Hilary introduced herself, and said she'd come about the pony.

'I'm Alison,' said the woman, 'and this is Lotte.' She put an arm around the girl's shoulders.

'Is it your pony?' Hilary asked gently.

Lotte nodded, blinking furiously. 'His name's Oscar.'

'He's kept at a yard just up the road,' Alison explained. 'It's a few minutes in the car.'

They piled into Alison's battered estate car, and Hilary smiled to herself at the familiarity of hay in the foot wells, and the jumble of coats and wellies.

Lotte sat in the back, and when Hilary glanced round, the girl was staring resolutely out of the window, biting her lip. Hilary felt for her. It was horrible growing out of a pony and having to sell it on. Like selling your best friend.

The yard was a tumbledown side-line to a farm. There was mud in the gateways, and none of the fencing looked very secure. To the right were the stables, and to the left, a large field, sloping down to some woodland in the distance. Half a dozen horses and ponies stood around the gate waiting to be brought in, while a half dozen more were dotted around the field, picking at the sparse grazing.

'There's Oscar,' said Lotte, leaning forward between the front seats and pointing. 'The grey.'

Hilary was surprised. Oscar was bigger than he'd looked in the photos. Easily big enough for this slip of a girl. So Lotte had not outgrown him then.

They climbed out of the car, and Lotte went to catch

Oscar, shooing the other ponies away from the gate. She brought him into the yard so Hilary could give him a proper look over.

'We should have brought him in earlier and cleaned him up a bit,' said Alison, ruefully.

'Oh, it's no problem,' said Hilary, rubbing Oscar's neck, and letting him give her a good sniff. 'Quite happy to see them in the rough.'

'We like to keep him out as much as possible,' said Alison. 'More natural for him than being stuck in the stable.'

'But he gets bullied,' said Lotte, stroking his nose gently. 'He's too much of a softy to stand up for himself.'

Oscar regarded Hilary with calm, brown eyes and his breath was warm against her hands. He was a lovely pony.

'How old did you say he was?'

'He's 18,' said Lotte.

'And he's sound and healthy?'

'Oh yes,' said Alison. 'Never been lame in all the time we've had him, and, touch wood – ' She tapped the stable door, 'he's never had the vet except for routine jabs.'

Hilary looked sideways at her. 'Then why are you selling him? Doesn't sound as if he ought to retire just yet.'

Alison sighed. 'Lotte's dad got made redundant last year, and he's found something else, but on a much smaller salary. We're only just covering the mortgage. We've tried for Lotte's sake to hold on, but last month they put the rent up here, and we simply can't afford it.'

'And there's nowhere cheaper for you to keep him?'

'We were offered a field to rent, but it's not practical. Here, there's someone to keep an eye on him on weekdays when Lotte's at school and I'm at work. If we just had a field, he'd be stuck on his own most of the time, and we're afraid he'd jump out or hurt himself.'

Hilary gazed at Lotte's tear-stained face and smiled. 'I might have a solution.'

'Do you think they'll make friends?' asked Lotte.

They had divided Hilary's paddock in two with a length of electric fence to give the ponies a chance to get to know each other before they went in together. Bramble stood resolutely as close to the fence as he dared, gazing at the new arrival, while Oscar walked around and around the boundaries of his new home. Occasionally, he paused to stretch out his nose timidly towards Bramble, but his nerve would always fail him at the last minute, and he'd wheel away and trot to the other side of the paddock, to begin pacing all over again.

'I'm sure they will,' said Hilary. 'It's a big change for both of them. Bramble hasn't lived with any pony other than Jasper for years. And Oscar's used to being in a big group. But they'll settle down. I'll keep an eye on them, don't you worry.'

'Thank you,' said Alison. The anxiety had left her face, and she smiled warmly at Hilary. 'Thank you so much – for all of this. It's perfect.'

'It's a pleasure. And don't forget, you're doing me a huge favour too – giving Bramble a new friend.'

'And you're sure you won't mind us coming and going, getting under your feet?' asked Alison.

Hilary shook her head. 'It'll be lovely to see some life about the place again.' She turned to Lotte. 'And remember, any time you want me to check on him, just let me know.'

Lottie had tears in her eyes again. But judging by her smile, this time they were good tears.

'Thank you!' she said. And to Hilary's surprise and joy, the little girl threw her arms around her and gave her a big hug.

It took a long time for Hilary to drop off to sleep that night. Despite her assurances that the ponies would be fine, she was alert to each hoof-beat, each snort or shake. Several times, she got up and peeked through her bedroom curtains, trying to make out if Oscar was settling OK.

When she finally slept, it was a restless night, filled with strange dreams.

The following morning, she woke with a start. It took her a moment to remember why her body was taut with anxiety. And then it came to her. Tumbling out of bed, she threw open the curtains. A chasm of dread opened up inside her. Oscar's side of the paddock was empty.

And then she laughed. The relief flowed through her, making her knees weak, and her breath come in great panting gasps.

The electric fence was on the floor. In the hazy morning sunshine, Oscar and Bramble were standing together, nose to tail, under the old willow tree. It was a beautiful sight; Oscar's sleek, grey coat contrasting with the cuddly, brown Bramble. She watched Oscar gently nibble the top of Bramble's tail, and in turn, Bramble rubbed his head against Oscar's hocks. They looked like old friends already.

There was the sound of a car in the lane and, a few moments later, Hilary heard the side gate open. Lotte came running into the garden, and across to the paddock fence. She turned and glanced up at Hilary's window and Hilary did a thumbs up sign. Lotte grinned and put both of her thumbs up too.

Hilary pulled on her dressing gown, listening to Lotte's delighted chatter as she pretended to give the ponies a good telling off for breaking through the electric fence.

She went downstairs, put the kettle on, and opened the kitchen window. Alison turned and waved.

'Cup of tea?' Hilary offered through the open window.

'That would be very kind,' Alison called back.

Hilary fetched mugs from the cupboard. She heard Lotte calling 'breakfast time' to the ponies, and Bramble's happy whinny as he saw the hay.

On the wall, the rosette ribbons fluttered in the breeze. Hilary's heart filled. It was almost like old times.

ONE FOR SORROW

Tash drove the grubby truck into the yard with the trailer behind clunking over the rutted concrete. She brought it to a gentle halt, silenced the engine, and climbed out.

Pete, lifting his head from the innards of a mud-splattered tractor, came out wiping his hands on an oily rag.

Tash nodded at the tractor. 'Having trouble?'

He made a face. 'It's like me - getting past it. It was running yesterday, but can't get it started today. Wasted the morning fiddling with the thing.'

She stood on tiptoe and gave him a kiss. His face was shockingly cold. 'Poor old thing.'

He didn't ask if she meant him or the tractor.

Behind them, there was a whinny from the trailer.

'Let's have a look at her then,' said Pete. His voice was grim. They were struggling as it was, and here was another mouth to feed. Not even a productive one.

Tash peered briefly through the jockey door, muttered a few soothing words, and then pulled down the front ramp. The piebald mare stared at them intently, her ears pitched forwards. Her back legs were splayed from keeping her balance in the box, but otherwise she looked unconcerned by the journey, simply interested to see where she had arrived. Tash untied the lead rope, released the breast bar and led the mare carefully down the ramp.

Pete said nothing, and Tash's heart sank. She knew that when he thought of horses, he imagined smart bay thoroughbreds - the sort you saw on telly lining up at the start of a race, sleek, as paired down and muscled as a whippet. But the mare was none of these things. Her coarse coat was made up of patches of black and white, like a furry monochrome map, and her legs were well feathered, so that she looked as if she was wearing 1970s style fluffy boots.

'She's a bit rough and ready now,' said Tash, 'but she'll soon scrub up.'

Pete ran a hand over his face. 'But she's not staying, right? This is just for a couple of months - then you're getting rid, yes?'

His tone made her want to cry with frustration. They'd discussed this over and over. OK, the farm wasn't doing well - what farm was right now? The market for livestock was sluggish, made worse by the perennial form-filling and bureaucracy. Thieves were targeting small farms like theirs where security was so difficult to maintain. Even the weather had been against them this year.

But she'd bought the mare for a song. At one of the livestock auctions, wiry, weather-beaten old Grimbatch, a permanent fixture at the sales, had sidled up to her and asked her if she was interested in a nag. The wily old guy had a few acres he rented out, and apparently he'd been left with the mare when the owner had disappeared without paying the rent. Tash had been dubious, until Grimbatch had produced the mare's passport, and a copy of the signed rental contract which did indeed state that livestock could be sold to recover unpaid debts. Grimbatch just wanted to cover the outstanding rent, and to be shot of the unwanted horse.

To Tash the situation was a gift. She would school the

mare over the next couple of months, take her to a few local indoor events over the winter, and then sell her when the show season got going in the spring. With any luck, there'd be a small profit she could then invest in a youngster of her own.

She took a deep breath and spoke evenly. 'That's the plan.'

'Good.'

'It's only fair after all.'

The words were out of her mouth before she'd had time to consider them. Pete looked at her, his eyes dark. 'I've made sacrifices too,' he said, and turned away back to the tractor.

Tash stood in the yard, staring at the mare. This hairy piebald cob couldn't replace Bailey, that was for sure. Bailey had been the most promising horse she'd ever owned, with his athletic limbs, his noble face, and his superb jumping ability. But Bailey had been sold last season to keep the farm afloat, and Tash did her best not to peer into the void his absence had created.

The mare watched her, placidly, her breath making little clouds in the sharp winter air as she examined Tash's hands and pockets for potential treats. Tash gave her a mint, and rubbed her between the ears. 'Not that you need anything else to eat - you're a tubby thing, aren't you?' At least she wasn't going to cost a lot to feed, thought Tash grimly. That would be one thing Pete wouldn't be able to grumble about.

'Come on then, lass,' said Tash softly. 'Let's pop you in your new box.'

She smiled to herself. She was looking forward to seeing a horse peering out from Bailey's empty stable.

'What've you done with the old nag that arrived yesterday?'

Pete rested his arms on the stable door and watched Tash as she fastened the straps on the mare's stable rug.

'Told you she'd scrub up alright!'

'I can't believe that's the same horse.'

The mare paused briefly from her haynet, flicked an ear at the sound of his voice, and wrinkled her nose a little as though she was mildly put out.

Pete laughed. It was a rich resonate sound - one which Tash had not heard in a long time.

'If I want her to be a successful riding club horse, the least I can do is make her look the part.'

The mare had behaved brilliantly throughout her transformation - standing statue still to have her coat bathed and clipped, putting up with Tash cursing when the clippers jammed in those thick feathery legs, and only once turning her head slightly indignantly when Tash had been tidying her long ragged mane and had pulled out a rather large knot. Now she stood, her white patches sparkling and her black patches gleaming.

'Can't you flog her like that?' asked Pete.

'Got to get this flab off first,' said Tash, patting the mare's tummy affectionately. 'Plenty of nice steady road work, and we'll soon have her looking a bit trimmer.'

'Stop feeding her then!' said Pete, nodding at the haynet from which the mare was tearing hay with concentration.

'You can't just starve them. It's like people - sensible diet and regular exercise.'

'S'pose.' Pete tipped his head on one side. 'By the way, what's her name?'

'Magpie, according to her passport.'

'Reckon Pork Pie would be more appropriate,' said Pete.

Tash made a face at the mare. 'Don't listen to the nasty man!'

She gave her a final pat before walking to the stable door and letting herself out. She was surprised when Pete pulled her into his arms. They stood together silently for a moment, before Pete said into her hair, 'I love you, you know. I know she's not Bailey, but if Pie makes you happy, then I'm happy she's here. OK?'

Tash nodded into his chest, and gave him a squeeze.

Then he lowered his voice and whispered, 'She's still going in the spring though!'

Tash gave him a pretend punch, and together they walked slowly back to the farm house.

It didn't matter that it was more work; having a horse again made her blood fizz with new found energy. Each day, she finished all her chores in record time, and made sure to do something with Pie. She worked her on the lunge and long reins, and found the mare to be calm and methodical in everything she did. She borrowed a treeless saddle from a friend which fitted Pie's broad back, and rode her around the farm for a few minutes every day. Her strides were short and choppy after Bailey's athletic pace, but she was willing and reasonably forward-going, only occasionally balking at passing some piece of strange farm machinery or a feed-bag flapping in the wind.

'We'll have to get you shod,' Tash told her, the first time they ventured out onto the lane. Pie's bare hooves sounded muffled on the tarmac. Tash tried to remember the last time she'd hacked out. It felt like a lifetime ago. All she and Pete ever seemed to do these days was work. Work, then sit in the kitchen, nursing mugs of tea, too exhausted to do anything else. Pie made a difference - Pie meant a tiny bit of the day belonged to Tash and Tash's personal dreams. Pie meant that not quite everything was about the farm.

She patted the mare's short chunky neck, and flipped an errant piece of mane back over to the right hand side. Pie shook her head, and the bit of mane flopped back to the left. Tash smiled to herself.

A small blue hatchback overtook them, very slowly and carefully. Tash recognised the old lady from the cottage at the end of the lane, and waved her a thank you. Pie glanced at the vehicle, but appeared unconcerned. When they passed the neighbouring farm, a telehandler was reversing in the yard. Pie stopped dead, head up, but Tash sat quietly, patted her, and then pushed her on, and that was that. Bailey would have objected in a much more dramatic fashion, Tash mused.

They didn't see another vehicle until they'd almost completed the loop of the lanes and were on their way back. A grey 4x4 coming the other way, slowed and pulled over. As they got closer the driver's window slid down, and Pie shied. Tash half expected the guy driving to say something, but he simply stared at them. Tash called out 'Thank you!' but there was no response. She pushed the hesitating Pie on with her legs, and they had a short jog-trot until the farm came into sight.

'How was that then, lass?' she said to the mare.

Pie snorted, and dropped her head, tugging for more rein.

'Longest ride yet,' said Tash, looking at her watch. 'Plenty more of that, and we'll soon have you a bit trimmer.'

But the weight was not coming off.

Tash stood gazing at the mare critically. If anything, Pie appeared to be even more rotund than she'd been when she arrived. Tash had loosened the straps on her stable rug the night before. 'But we've hacked out for miles over the last few weeks,' Tash muttered, 'and I'm being so careful with your rations.' Pie was pulling frantically at her haynet. That was the other thing - she always seemed ravenous. Of course, horses were pretty greedy, but even so. She'd started chewing the wood panels which lined the stable walls. Perhaps she needed a supplement. Maybe she ought to ask the vet for advice. More expense to send Pete off muttering.

Then a horrible thought stuck her.

'She's what?' Pete dropped his fork onto his dinner plate

and stared at Tash.

'In-foal.'

'You are kidding me?'

Tash shook her head without meeting his eye.

'The vet said she'll be due around the end of February.'

'So this mare you bought as a little money making enterprise - you won't be able to work her any longer, she's actually going to cost us a fortune in vet bills, and then we'll have two mouths to feed?'

Tash nodded. Unsurprisingly, she had already considered each of these implications.

'Not to mention the fact that we're bringing another unwanted, badly bred coloured cob foal into the world when there's already thousands of horses out there worth next to nothing.'

Tash looked up. 'That's not fair. I didn't know she was pregnant when I bought her, and she's a nice quality mare - you've no idea what the stallion was like, so you can't know what the foal will be like.'

'That's rot,' said Pete, pushing his plate away. 'You know as well as I do the kind of life horses like that have - running half-feral in a big herd with a load of other mongrels. You know exactly the kind of foal she's likely to have.' He stood up abruptly. 'You want to get on to that swindler Grimbatch - demand your money back, and tell him he can have the hassle of looking after a pregnant horse.'

He stormed out of the kitchen, and Tash heard the back door slam behind him.

She sat at the table staring at her half-eaten dinner. Pete was wrong about one thing. Shocked as she was to find Pie was in foal, the last thing she wanted to do was attempt to get her money back.

The truth was, this was the first glimmer of excitement they'd had in their lives for far too long.

Tash watched the red digits of her alarm clock glowing in

the dark. Something had woken her, and she held her breath for a moment to listen. There was nothing, and then downstairs in the kitchen, she heard Millie, the old collie-cross, whimper.

Tash unplugged her mobile phone from its charger, and using the glow from the screen to guide her way, slipped out of bed. The dog couldn't always make it through the night now. Pete was all for leaving her in the barn, but Millie was a sweet old thing, and Tash didn't like the idea of her being outside on a freezing winter night. That said, the last thing she needed was the dog waking Pete. He was bad tempered enough these days even after a full night's sleep.

She padded downstairs, and fetched a coat and woolly hat from the back of the kitchen door. The kitchen was bathed in moonlight, bright enough to see Millie wag her tail feebly. Tash pushed her feet into wellies over her pyjama bottoms, and opened the back door.

For a second, she thought she heard an engine. She held her breath. Nothing. Millie nosed the air. It was a sharp, clear night; stars twinkled in the inky blackness, and a cool moon hung behind the trees.

Last year someone had tried to break in and steal the red diesel from the tank at the back of the barn. They'd had a security light installed afterwards, and for a while had been super vigilant, joining the local Farm Watch group and sharing info. But things had gone quiet recently, and they'd got out of the habit. Stupid really.

Tash's heart began to thump. The night air seemed expectant somehow. She listened again. In the field to the left, next to the lane, the sheep were moving uneasily; a chorus of baaing. In a low voice she called to Millie, and they set off, slipping through the gate and heading across the field. There might be a fox, and if that was it, Millie would see it off.

Millie kept at Tash's heels as they crossed the damp ground. The sheep had moved over to the far side of the field, away from the lane. They'd come together in a ragged huddle and were turned to stare in Tash's direction. In the moonlight, it was all too easy to see why. There was a truck and stock trailer parked in the lane.

Tash swore under her breath. They were after the bloody sheep. She fumbled in her pocket for her phone, and logged a call with the Police. Not that it would do much good. Last year, the Police had taken 40 minutes to get to the neighbouring farm - by which time someone had already nicked a tractor. No, Tash would have to act. The thieves would take the sheep through the old gate further up. It was padlocked, but they'd probably have bolt cutters. She started to jog. The only thing would be to try to scare them off. She was glad of the dog, even if Millie was too old to be of any real use. The thieves wouldn't know that.

But when Tash reached the gate, and peered gingerly into the lane, it was deserted. She climbed over, while Millie squeezed through the bars, and crept up to the truck. It was a dark coloured 4x4 - grey, perhaps? There was no-one inside.

Perhaps they didn't know about the gate? That would explain why the truck was facing the other way, the trailer facing towards the farm. Even now, they might be at the front gate, trying to get to the sheep that way.

She rang Pete's phone but there was no answer. He'd started putting it on 'do not disturb' because he was such a rubbish sleeper.

So she was on her own. What to do?

She contemplated letting the tyres down, but her nerve failed her. Instead, she took a couple of photos of the truck and trailer, including the registration numbers of each. They didn't match, and it was possible they were fake, but it was better than nothing. Then, still clutching her phone, she had another idea. She started to jog as quietly as she could towards the main farm gates. Definitely thieves - the gate chain was on the floor and the left hand gate had been pushed open. Keeping close to the hedge, she peered into the yard. Nothing. She ran across the gateway and, pressing herself as far into the hedge on the opposite side as she could, she cued up the YouTube clip she needed, turned up the volume on her phone as high as it would go, and hit play.

The sound of a Police siren filled the air, urgent and wailing.

Within seconds a tall, gangly youth in a hoodie shot out of the gate. Millie chased after him barking frantically, and the guy leapt into the 4x4, started the engine and drove away, the trailer bumping and clanging behind it. The collie stood in the lane, barking, as though saying, 'Yeah, be off with you!'

Tash turned off the siren sound effect, and the silence rushed in. Was that more footsteps? No, she must have imagined it. She pushed herself out of the hedge, and went through the gates, glancing up at the farm house. A light went on in their bedroom. Pete's face appeared at the window for a second, and then he was gone. She pulled the gates closed behind her, and then she heard something else.

She flew into the yard, and stopped short. The mare, wearing a head collar with the lead rope trailing on the floor, was grazing at the bottom of the hedgerow by the sheep field.

Pete came running towards her from the house. 'What's going on? Are you OK?'

Tash picked up the end of the trailing lead rope and turned towards Pete, frowning.

'I think someone just tried to steal Pie!'

'Blimey! What a night!'

Pete gazed into his third cup of coffee and shook his head.

The Police had been and gone. Tash had shared the photos from her phone, and they been amused by her sound effect stunt.

'I just assumed they were after the sheep,' said Tash, for the umpteenth time.

'That Grimbatch!' said Pete. 'It's his fault.' He looked up at Tash. 'And yours too - you fool, for buying the bloody mare off him!' He got up suddenly and came round to her side of the table, crouched and put his arms around her. 'You don't know how scared I was when those bloody sirens went off and I found you weren't in bed, and there were people running and the dog barking. I imagined all kinds of horrors.' He buried his head in her lap. 'I mean, you're still an idiot, but you're my idiot, and I don't want to lose you!'

She grinned and stroked his hair. 'I wasn't in any danger.' She paused. 'Hang on, did you say "people running"? Don't exaggerate. There was only one guy!'

He lifted his head. 'Sounded like more than one to me.'

Tash shrugged. 'You probably heard Pie by walking under your window!'

'Probably.'

There was no point in going back to bed. They started on with the day, adrenalin keeping them going through the lack of sleep. Tash fed Millie, and went to let out the hens. Pete went to the barn to see to the ewes who were closest to lambing. Tash went out to fill the feed trough for the sheep in the field, then she put Pie in the paddock behind the barn, and started mucking out. It was when she was wheeling the barrow to the muck heap that she spotted a slim youth standing by the fence. Pie had gone over to him; head over the fence, snuffling happily at the pockets of his grubby hoody.

'Excuse me!' Tash was aware her voice had come out haughty and supercilious.

The youth flashed her a glance, and then bolted. By the time she'd followed him round the back of the barn, there was no sign of him.

People running, Pete had said.

Tash stood with her hands on her hips and stared at Pie. 'Someone wants you back pretty badly.'

She didn't say anything to Pete about the youth. Didn't want another barrage of criticism for buying Pie in the first place. But she was more vigilant over the next few days. And she padlocked the gate to Pie's field.

Pie was bulbous now. Tash was reading everything she could find on the care of pregnant mares. She'd bought extra feed which she'd hidden in a bin in the outhouse by the stable. The responsibility of bringing a foal safely into the world made her feel faintly sick when she thought about it. So she tried not to.

Mainly she blocked out her worries by working. Fortunately, there was lots of work. And in the lambing pens, the sound of baaing drowned out all thought anyway. She and Pete stank of sheep. They worked like automatons and did little more than grunt at one another.

After lambing the previous year, they had talked about getting someone in to help this year. Most people they knew had parents or siblings who could be called on in an emergency, but Pete and Tash were first generation farmers; Pete's parents lived in sheltered accommodation, and Tash's were city dwellers who, whilst enjoying a stay at the farm in the summer months, couldn't really be expected to stay up all hours on a freezing February night. Besides, Tash doubted they'd be much help even if they were here.

So when, about a week later, after another sleepless night, Tash dragged herself to Pie's stable ready to muck out, she thought she was hallucinating when she found the stable door propped open and the wheelbarrow jammed in the doorway.

The youth was wearing a different grubby hoody today. He paused, the shavings fork poised over the wheelbarrow. Behind him, Pie was tucking into a net of hay.

'What do you think you're doing?' Tash asked. Her voice was laced with exhaustion. She could not face this.

'Helping,' said the youth. He tipped the fork-load of muck into the barrow.

Tash leaned against the door frame and shut her eyes. 'Why?'

'Because Maggie is mine.'

Maggie. Tash smiled in spite of herself. Maggie was a nicer pet name for the mare than bloody Pie!

'I'm not joking,' said the youth. 'I mean it - she's mine.'

The sincerity in his voice made her open her eyes again. His face was flushed, his eyes dark with emotion. Now she was able to study him closely, it was clear he was younger than she'd first thought. Little more than a boy.

'I bought her,' she said, 'I've got a receipt and her passport.'

'You bought her from a thief!' he answered hotly.

'He told me he took her in place of an unpaid debt.'

The boy worked his lips. 'He told *me* he was going to give me time to pay - and then he didn't. Just sold her without telling me.'

'And you tried to steal her back?'

'What? No!' I came the other day to see her, that's all. I ran because I thought you'd take one look at me and assume the worst - and I was right too, wasn't I?'

Tash pursed her lips. 'You can see how it looked to me. Particularly after the other night.'

The boy looked at her sideways. 'Dunno what you mean.'

'What, you didn't come here with a trailer one night last week, and try to steal her back?'

'No! Where would I get a trailer from? I can't even drive!'

'There was another man - skinny like you, but tall.'

The boy's eyes widened in fear. 'Nothing to do with me.' He moved closer to the mare and dropped his arm over her back protectively. 'Maggie's mine. No-one else's.'

'Well, someone else thinks otherwise,' said Tash.

Pete leaned against the range cooker, arms folded across his chest. Exhaustion etched his face, but his expression still managed to be thunderous.

'The thing is, how do you expect us to trust you?'

The boy was silent, sullen under scrutiny.

Tash made a face at her husband. 'Grimbatch went back on his word. Connor thought they had an agreement.'

'So he says.'

'We did!' Connor protested hotly. 'He said I could work her rent. But he wanted me there all hours. Made me do all kinds of filthy stuff. He was taking the piss.'

'So you just stopped working for him?'

'No, I broke my bloody arm. I was in plaster for six weeks. Told him. Said I'd do double shifts after - which was a joke since I was already doing stupid hours. But he didn't wait. He just sold her, didn't he? I went every day to check on her. One day, she'd gone.'

'And you found out where, and came to steal her back?' Pete's voice was harsh.

'No!' Connor got up so quickly, he almost toppled the kitchen chair.

Tash put her hand up. 'That wasn't him,' she said to Pete.

'Yeah, right!' Pete snapped.

'It wasn't!' Connor protested. 'First time I was here was the other day,' he pointed at Tash, 'when she saw me.'

Pete turned on Tash. 'You saw him on our property days ago and never said anything?'

'He was standing chatting to Pie - he wasn't doing anything.'

Pete smacked his forehead theatrically. 'I don't bloody believe it. After we had an attempted robbery in the night?'

'That wasn't me!' Connor repeated.

Pete rounded on him. 'But you know who it was, don't

you?'

They both stared at the boy. The colour was high in his cheeks.

'It was probably one of my uncle's lads.'

'And your uncle is?' Pete asked.

'An arsehole you don't want to know,' said Connor. 'Horse dealer. Does a bit of breeding. I used to keep Maggie at his place - free because I was family. She had a little paddock out of the way. It was fine. Then his bloody stallion got out - savaged her. Bit and kicked her, she was lame on one hind leg - a right mess. That's why I moved her.'

'And how she ended up in foal,' said Tash.

Connor looked down. 'I wasn't sure about that - but yeah.'

'What's this stallion like?' asked Pete.

'That's the thing - he's not normally vicious,' said Connor. 'He was always dead good to handle, but something got into him that one night.'

'That's not what I was getting at,' said Pete. 'What I mean is - and no disrespect to Pie, or Maggie or whatever you call her - but they didn't come here to steal a coloured cob. They came for the foal.'

'Oh yeah,' said Connor, nodding enthusiastically. 'He's quality.'

Pete looked at Tash and suddenly grinned. 'Looks like you got yourself a bargain after all!'

Tash looked back at Pete, blinking in shock. Then she too smiled. 'And I think I've got a plan which will keep everyone happy.'

A moment of calm prevailed in the lambing shed. They were all fed and watered and, other than the odd bleat from a new lamb, all appeared content. Pete, who had kept watch most of the night, had gone to grab a nap. Tash sipped at the coffee she'd brought out in a thermos, and allowed herself to relax slightly. Another couple of weeks, and it would be over, this feeling of being constantly drugged with exhaustion.

In the nearest pen, a new lamb staggered to its feet, and wobbled over to its mother. In spite of everything, Tash felt a glow of joy at this new life. It never ceased to amaze her. Yes, it was their business, and yes, it was bloody hard work. But this - this made it all worth it.

She watched Connor throw his leg over a hurdle, and come to claim a coffee. Despite no previous experience with sheep, having him here had been a godsend. He learned fast and the simple relief of having an extra pair of hands had been incredible. The work - and sleep - could be shared three ways, and now the majority of the lambing was over, a huge weight had been lifted from their shoulders. Even Pete had to admit the arrangement was a good one - though his was an uneasy alliance with the boy.

'Cheers,' Connor said, accepting the coffee with his left hand. He flexed his right arm and winced.

'Hurting?' asked Tash.

Connor shrugged. 'Just aches a bit now and then.'

'Well, we're done for now. Give it a rest for a couple of hours, hey?' She doubted he would. He was a hard worker. 'How did you break it?'

Connor's gaze shifted to the middle distance. 'At my uncle's place. We were fetching down some hay bales. Fell off the stack.'

'Ouch.' Tash thought for a moment. 'So, that would have been when you were working for Grimbatch too? You were working two jobs?'

'Wasn't really working for my uncle by then, but I was living in a little caravan on his place, so, you know - he expected me to help.'

'Even after what had happened to Maggie?' said Tash softly, 'And you having to move her?'

'Yeah, he wasn't happy about that.' Connor stared into his coffee.

'You couldn't have wanted to be there, surely? Couldn't

you have gone home?'

A shadow passed over Connor's face. 'Nah, mum said she'd washed her hands of me after I went to my uncle's place. She and him don't get on.'

'How come?'

Connor gave a grimace. 'She just knows what he's like. She warned me, but...'

'But you wanted to be with the horses, so you thought you'd take the risk?'

Connor nodded. 'And then I got Maggie, so, you know - I had to stay.'

Tash tried to imagine what it must have been like for the lad, living in a caravan, keeping his head down, and looking after his piebald cob, at his uncle's dealer yard.

She reached out and took hold of his right wrist. Connor flinched. There was a small bump where it looked like the bone had not set quite right.

'Fell off a hayrick,' she said. 'Is that what you told them in A&E?'

Connor's dark brown eyes met hers; deep pools of pain. He said nothing.

Tash had been up twice already in the night, slipping silently from the farmhouse, and padding down to the yard. Each time, when she had peered into the stable, she found Connor, wrapped in a sleeping bag, keeping watch. She'd told him to go to bed, but he just shook his head, and carried on watching the mare.

The third time she came down, the boy was asleep in the corner of the box. Magpie stood, watchful and still. There was a slight glisten to her coat, but otherwise there was no sign of any immediate action.

Tash found Connor's dedication to Magpie difficult to credit. It made her love of Bailey look feeble in comparison. She'd hardly fought for him at all when it came down to it. Yet this boy had moved into the back room of the farm house, and was working his bed, board, and Magpie's original purchase price. They had agreed - he would have her back once the foal was weaned.

She went back into the kitchen. Millie, lying by the range, thumped her tail in greeting but did not move. Tash poured herself a glass of milk and sat at the kitchen table. She would have preferred tea but couldn't be bothered to put the kettle on. She probably ought to try to sleep, but despite the fog of exhaustion, she knew she would just lie there, watching the red digits on her alarm clock click forward.

The last few weeks had been tough. Tash had constantly fretted about the mare's welfare. She'd kept horses for years, but she'd never looked after an expectant mum before. And the fact that the foal might be something special just made the responsibility worse.

She'd fallen into a semi doze, leaning on one arm on the table, when Millie sat up suddenly.

Tash lifted her head. Had there been a noise?

She grabbed the nearest coat, which was one of Pete's, and let herself out of the back door, Millie at her heels.

The wind was buffeting the trees, making dead leaves swirl and tumble across the yard. The gates were open. Tash stiffened, and pulled her phone from the pocket of her fleece. She could hear voices. Connor and another man. A wave of doubt washed over her. Had Connor sold her a pack of lies? Was blood thicker than water when it came down to it?

But when she crept around the corner to Maggie's stable, the doubts disappeared. The security light had come on, illuminating the two figures perfectly.

Connor, barring the way to Maggie's stable, armed with only a shavings fork, was shouting, 'She's not yours - she was never yours - so stay away from her!'

'Or what?' Connor's uncle was huge, a bear of a man. 'You think I'm afraid of you? My sister's runt! Just get the mare out, and let's get going.'

'I don't work for you anymore, I don't have to do what

you say,' said Connor defiantly.

'Yeah you do - or do you want me to break your other arm? Remember how easy that was?'

'I think you'll find that's GBH.' Tash's voice rang out across the yard.

Connor and his Uncle both swung round to face her.

Tash kept her phone aloft, recording it all.

'I think the Police will be very interested in both your threatened violence - which I believe is classed as common assault,' she went on, her voice high and clear and icy. 'Along with your admission of a previous act of GBH, which will have been documented by A&E.'

For a moment the three of them remained frozen in the glow of the security light. Then with incredible speed for a large man, Connor's uncle came for her.

In that moment, Tash knew real terror. Her body responded too slowly to her brain's order to flee. She turned and ran, but he was right behind her. Inevitably, his hand grabbed at her. She threw one arm back behind her and twisted as she ran, and the huge old coat, which she'd never had time to fasten, slid off leaving Connor's uncle clutching at the fabric.

And then there was a grunt, a yelp and a cry.

He wasn't behind her any longer.

She slowed, glanced back and ran straight into another man. She screamed.

'Whoa....I've got you!' said Pete, 'You're OK.'

'Jesus!' Tash turned, her heart pounding, her chest heaving. 'Connor's uncle - I thought *he'd* got me.'

They turned, and Pete began to laugh. 'It's alright - I think he fell over the dog.'

It was a beautiful sight: Connor standing over his uncle, who was struggling to sit up, cradling one arm against his chest.

'It's just like you told me that time,' Connor said, 'Natural reflex to put your arm out to break your fall.' He shook his head. 'Hurts, doesn't it?'

In the distance, they could hear a siren.

'Sounds like this one's for real!' said Tash, head tipped, listening.

'Oh yeah,' said Pete. 'I called the police - and they made us a priority since we've had trouble recently.'

Tash and Connor leaned over the stable door and gazed at the tiny foal who was already attempting to stand on ungainly stick thin legs.

'You are a clever girl,' Tash said to Magpie, 'you did this all by yourself - while all that was going on outside. You didn't need us after all, did you?'

The mare gazed at her with liquid brown eyes.

'Tash, Connor!' Pete called from behind them, 'the Police need your statements.'

'Shush!' said Tash, and beckoned him over.

'Oh, my - oh! What a beauty!' Pete's voice went soft, his eyes fixed on the foal. 'What an absolute beauty.'

The foal was almost all black. He had bright white stockings on each leg, as though someone had dipped him deeply in white paint, and his tail was shot through with white hair so it appeared almost silver in the soft stable light. Otherwise, the only indication of his piebald parentage was a single blob of white, like a small cloud, on his left side. His head was fine and there was a white star between his beautiful dark eyes.

'Isn't he perfect?' said Tash, glancing up at Pete.

Pete nodded his head slowly in wonder. 'He certainly is.'

'Maggie's gonna make a great mum,' said Connor. 'Look.'

They watched the mare nibbling at the foal's coat, encouraging it to take its first steps and find her milk.

Tears sprang into Tash's eyes. 'You know you can carry on keeping her here, don't you?' she said to Connor.

'Thanks, I'd like that.' Connor picked at a strand of horse hair caught in the door.

'And we'll discuss proper wages if you want to stay on?' suggested Pete.

Connor grinned. 'Yeah, I'd like that too. Be really good.'

'On one condition,' said Tash gently.

Connor looked at her.

'Think you ought to get in touch with your mum, don't you?' Tash watched him steadily.

Connor nodded.

'Then it's a deal.'

The first rays of weak morning sunlight crept across the yard, and the birds began to sing in the trees. A tiny glimpse of spring on the horizon. A tiny glimmer of hope ahead.

The foal staggered a couple of steps, his nose bumping against Magpie's flank, and then he latched on to his mother, his little silver tail shaking with contentment.

Two horses at the farm.

Oh yes, definitely a glimmer of hope ahead. Hope, and joy.

NOT THE HORSE FOR ME?

I wedged my pen into the top of my clipboard and lay the whole thing on the grass. Above me, birds were chirruping in the trees, intermittently drowned out by the cars swooshing past on the nearby road.

Kath pulled her thermos out of the car, rested the lid on the bonnet and said, 'Want some?'

'Nah,' I said. 'I'll only end up needing a wee.'

'Plenty of bushes!'

'Uh-huh - and knowing my luck, the minute I drop my trousers there'll be a cavalcade of riders!'

Kath and I were acting as road stewards for a charity pleasure ride. We'd been assigned the busy road crossing because a) from the side the riders were approaching, it was tricky to see around the bend, and b) the path they needed to follow on the other side was a dog-leg and not easy to make out.

Kath pulled her phone from her pocket. 'Half past one. Should be just the final few now I guess, if they all went out by noon.'

We'd done this stewarding business several times before so we knew the drill. First to go had been a couple of keen endurance types on super-fit Arabs. They'd whizzed around the entire ride in about 40 minutes, shouting their numbers to us as they flew by. Then we'd had a boring wait for the first of the 'happy hackers'. Today's wait was especially long as the first group had got lost en route, and several other groups had ended up following them. Just when we were starting to get really worried, they all arrived together, all talking at once, all attempting to regale us with tall tales of missed markers and helpful-not-helpful dog walkers who had led them down the wrong path.

Attempting to see this group of about 14 riders safely across the road was a challenge - especially with all of them talking at once, and no-one watching out for their own safety. I feared they were expecting our fluorescent tabards to act as a magic talisman against the speeding traffic, but somehow they got across safely.

After that there was a steady run of well-spaced groups of two, three or four horses and riders, who each arrived under control, smiling and grateful for our help, and Kath and I beamed beatifically. Then there was another lull.

'Don't you wish it was you?' asked Kath, squinting at me against the sunshine.

'Was me what?'

'Riding - not stuck here stewarding.'

I shrugged. 'I've done it all before. And you were tail-end-Charlie at the last ride, so you can't grumble.'

Kath stuck out her tongue at me and stretched her long slender limbs. 'I know, I know. That's why I offered to steward this time. But all those noble aspirations about giving back to the equestrian community kind of go out the window when you're actually stuck here for hours on such a glorious day, and that track up there looks so perfect for a canter.' She glanced dreamily up the dog-legged path into the distance. 'It's not fair - when I was tail-end-Charlie it was peeing down and the paths were all churned up by the time we went round.'

'Poor, poor Kath. How unlucky you are - if only you

had a beautiful and talented horse....oh wait - you do!'

Kath threw a pebble at me and grinned. 'You're not tempted to get another one?'

I allowed this thought to skitter over the surface of my mind and plop into the deep dark recesses without pausing to give it any consideration.

'Nah, I'm fine just doing this sort of stuff. I like watching other people enjoying themselves and without people like me, they couldn't do this sort of thing.'

'Doesn't stop you getting another horse though,' Kath reasoned. 'You could still do good deeds even as a horse owner.'

'I know, but I really don't want to take on another one,' I said firmly. 'Not after Bobby.' I picked up my clipboard and said, 'Riders!'

There were two horses coming down the track towards us; a skewbald cob in front with a tumbling mane and incredibly clean feathers, and behind him a palomino.

My heart stopped. The palomino was about 15.2hh with elegant, slender legs. It had sweated up considerably over its neck and shoulders but this didn't detract from the fact it might possibly have been the most beautiful horse I had ever seen - I mean in real life, close-up, as opposed to on the telly or in those Instagram photos which have had a kazillion filters applied.

I plastered on my best smile and walked up to greet them.

'Hi! How are you guys doing so far? Enjoying yourselves?'

'*I* am,' said the woman on the skewbald cob. 'I'm having a lovely time enjoying the gorgeous scenery. I don't think my daughter's having much fun though - bloody animal!'

I noted her number and turned to the second rider, who rolled her eyes theatrically.

'She's been an utter nightmare all the way round.' The daughter was slim and elegant, a perfect match for her beautiful horse. 'I dunno what's up with her. She wasn't like this when we bought her.'

I walked beside them, reached out and put my hand on the mare's sweaty neck. She was breathing hard through flared nostrils, the insides showing red and livid.

'How long have you had her?'

'About three months. She was fine to begin with. My mum thinks the dealer was dodgy - like she was drugged or something, and once it wore off she started acting like this.'

'She looks pretty hot,' I ventured. 'Do you want to stand and catch your breath for a sec?'

'She won't!' said the girl. She looked close to tears, and gathered another handful of sweat-soaked rein. 'She's just pulled and pulled the whole way round.'

The skewbald had reached the road so there was nothing for me to do but look for a gap in the traffic and see them safely across.

I watched Kath gesturing up the dog-leg path and explaining the route beyond, and then they headed off, the mare bouncing and trembling behind the cob.

'Blimey, that looked a bit of a handful,' said Kath.

But I found I couldn't answer.

We pulled back into the car park next to the secretary's tent, which was actually a borrowed gazebo, and started dragging the ride signage and so forth out of Kath's car. The last few riders were collecting their rosettes and comparing saddle-sore bottoms and stirrup-leather-rubbed legs. Kath and I grabbed a left-over sandwich each and flopped down on the grass.

'Brilliant day, ladies,' said Debs, the event organiser. '136 riders in total - everyone seems to have enjoyed themselves. Put some more people in touch with the bridleways group. Nice total for the charity, and once this last lot get off we should be good to go home and enjoy the rest of the weekend.'

'Amen to that,' said Kath. 'Though I'd not count on that pair getting away any time soon.'

I followed her gaze. In the distance I could see a green horse trailer with one pony on board and another standing on the ramp refusing to load. It was the palomino mare. As we watched, someone came over with a lunge line, attached it to one side of the trailer, lay it behind the mare's quarters and began to pull. The line slipped down a little to just above the horse's hocks where upon she reared, slipped and somersaulted over backwards.

'Oh my life!' Debs exclaimed.

But I was already on my feet and running.

The mare was struggling in the tangle of line and lead rope. She scrambled to her feet, flanks heaving. The mother shouted 'Grab her quick,' but when the daughter dived for the lead rope, the mare threw up her head, the muscles in her haunches gathered and then she was away.

It was pure fluke that as I was running towards them, the mare ran at me, and that I managed to grab her lead rope as her shoulder cannoned into me. I stumbled, but held on, and she did a pirouette around me before coming to a halt. Her eyes, wide with fear, met mine.

'It's OK, little lady,' I said, rather stupidly since it was fairly obvious everything was far from OK in her world. I laid a hand on her lathered neck, and scratched up under her mane, waiting for her to calm a little, but she wasn't having any of it, and stalked another circle around me.

'OK, so shall we walk a bit?' I said, and set off on a bigger circle, letting her walk out her panic. 'There's the lass,' I muttered, and an ear flicked toward me.

'Oh my God!' The teenage daughter was bounding towards us like a gazelle. 'Are you OK? Thank you so much for catching her. Oh God, what am I going to do? I'm never going to get her loaded.'

'No,' I said, 'I really don't think you are - not today.'

The girl pulled her phone out of her pocket. 'And I have to be at work this evening. I'm supposed to be back already to get changed.' She started stabbing the screen. She had long, acrylic nails, beautifully painted, and I was struck by how she'd managed not to damage them during the ride.

'How far have you come?' I asked.

'Not far.' The girl tossed her shiny raven hair (apparently unaffected by having been squashed under a sweaty hat for hours) and said, 'But you saw what she was like on the ride - I can't hack back.'

'Could you walk her - I mean, just lead her home?'

'I dunno. I don't know the way. Mum knows.' She gestured vaguely towards her mother who was standing, hands on hips, talking to the woman who'd had the misguided lunge line idea.

I looked at the beautiful mare and something inside me crystallised. I found myself saying, 'If you let me know where I'm supposed to be taking her, I'll walk her back.'

The girl looked at me as if she might genuinely sob with relief.

'You are raving mad,' Kath pronounced, arms folded across her chest.

'Not at all,' I said. 'Their yard is only about three miles away if we go across country, and down the back lanes. We'll be back before it's dark.'

'What if you get lost?'

I rolled my eyes. 'I've lived here all my life. I know the area. We'll be fine.'

She made the sort of noise my dad would have made if he'd been alive to witness my folly, and said, 'Well, have you at least got enough phone battery? Call me when you get there and I'll come and pick you up.'

'Thanks mate!' I said, and grinned at her.

'Barking!' she said, shaking her head. But I wondered if there was a tiny bit of admiration too. I didn't do mad things. I was Mrs Sensible. Usually.

We'd swapped the mare's headcollar for her bridle, so

I'd have a bit more control and could safely lead on the roads, and removed all her bandages and her travel rug, so she was just a horse again. I still had on my 'Please pass wide and slow' tabard, and I'd found some gloves. Debs made me wear a hard hat she had in her car, since from all that we'd witnessed, the mare was likely to be a handful.

The ramp went up on the green trailer (I'm sure it was my imagination, but the mare seemed to let out a sigh of relief as soon as she saw this), and the mother, who'd given me the destination postcode for my map app, sat behind the wheel of her truck, evidently eager to be off.

I got as close as I could and called across, 'By the way, what's the mare's name?'

'Callie,' she called back. 'Short for Supercalifragilistic!'

I looked at the mare and the mare looked back at me and I said, 'Blimey!' The inner child in me had expected her to be called something romantic like Firefly.

'OK, Callie,' I said, 'Let's get you home!'

Everything was fine to begin with. Callie seemed completely zoned out now that the twinned threats of climbing into a horse box or being ridden had been removed. She moved with an effortless fluidity which was a joy to behold, her limbs floating over the ground in the way of racehorses in the parade ring on the telly. I tried to give her plenty of free rein, partly because I wanted to be able to stand back and admire her, but also because I didn't want her to feel I was nagging at her all the time. If she was wondering who the hell I was, it didn't register in her demeanour.

The first part of our journey took us over some of the ride route, so we were following lots of previous hoof prints. Fortunately by now it was quieter, and we only saw a couple of dog walkers. No-one made a comment about why I was taking my horse out for a walk, though I saw a couple of strange glances in our direction.

And I was relieved. I would have been oddly embarrassed to talk to people, for them to mistake her for being mine. It was alright for that slip of a teenager who'd been riding her - she was exactly the sort of person who should own a horse like Callie - what with the long hair, stunning make-up, and nice nails. Callie and the girl were a matched pair - both capable of turning heads. Me, I was just ordinary. My equestrian life had been full of sensible cobs, all worth their weight in gold, but not in the same class.

Like Bobby. Dear Bobby who I'd lost a couple of years previously. He'd been level headed and versatile, and we'd done all sorts in our time together. But he hadn't had Callie's athleticism, bless him. He'd been like me, sensible and careful. Could turn a hoof to all sorts, but never excelled in anything. I'd loved him because he was my friend and I knew he'd look after me.

This creature walking beside me was something else. It was all a little unreal - though I was guessing the following day my muscles would be telling me just how real it had been.

As we walked, I ran my hands down her neck, scratching her under her mane, and laughing when she made comical faces of pleasure. I scratched over her withers which she also enjoyed, but when I reached her back, she flinched. And suddenly her behaviour on the ride made sense. Not hot-headed and difficult - merely in pain.

After we left the ride route, we took an unmade road through a bank of woodland. I began to realise that my confident assertion that I knew the area like the back of my hand was misplaced. Callie, possibly picking up on my uncertainty, became increasingly spooky, and I was grateful for my gloves as she snatched at the reins, and grateful for my hat when a bird flew out of the bushes and Callie did a mini-rear, front legs waving dangerously near my face for a moment. Each demonstration of fear, or perhaps challenge, I attempted to ignore. I just waited for her to stop, and carried on steadily.

I could feel my heart starting to race. I'd lost signal on

my phone, so I wasn't convinced the map app was telling me the truth any longer. What if I got us both lost? What if Callie's behaviour got worse?

I started to sing to myself. Inevitably, I sang 'Supercalifragilisticexpialidocious'. Fake it until you make it, they say. I was going to fake being confident. Fake being the sort of person who could have a horse like this one.

It was all going really well, and then we came to a sudden halt.

Instead of getting to the end of the woodland and finding more fields as I'd expected, I discovered I'd brought us to a housing estate. I was going to have to lead the mare through maze of winding roads!

And yet the mare didn't seem unduly perturbed. She regarded the houses and the parked cars with indifference, and flicked her ears towards the distant sound of a lawn mower.

Just then a woman who'd been crouched down in her front garden stood up. Callie spooked and then, spying a bucket of tasty looking weeds in her hand, looked at the woman enquiringly.

'Oopsy!' said the woman brightly, 'Sorry to make you jump. We don't get many horses around here!'

I looked at her sheepishly. 'I'm sure there didn't use to be houses here. Last time I was here, all this was fields.'

The woman gave a delighted laugh. 'Well, we've been here for over 10 years, so you've not been here for a while.'

Ten years! Had I really not noticed this whole rambling estate? As a kid we'd ridden around here. In fact, I was pretty sure I'd brought Bobby around here in our early days.

'That's a beautiful horse,' the woman added.

'Isn't she?'

'You're very lucky to have her.'

'Oh, she's not mine!' I replied hastily, feeling myself blush.

'Really? You might want to tell her that!'

The mare was rubbing her forehead against my arm and nudging me as if to say 'We can't stand around here chatting all day!'

I mentioned the address of the yard I was heading for, and the woman pointed down the labyrinth of estate roads and described the way as best she could. Now we were back in suburbia, the phone app reconnected, so I said goodbye and then Callie and I were on our way.

'Fancy her thinking you were mine - a posh bird like you,' I said to Callie.

The horse dropped her muzzle into my hand and blew gently, as if saying, 'S'alright.'

Walking Callie through the estate was surprisingly moving. In a stretch of tiny bungalows, an elderly man sitting in a chair by his window waved at us with a big smile on his face. Two children came charging out of their house, mum in tow, apologetically asking if it was OK to say hello to the horsey and give her a carrot. And bless her, Callie was a star and chewed her treat politely while the kids stroked her neck and asked a hundred questions about her - most of which I couldn't answer.

By now the best of the daylight was fading from the sky and we had to cross a busy road before heading up a lane on the other side. We passed a small holding with a barking dog, and Callie barely glanced at it, as if saying 'how rude!'

The battery on my phone was getting quite low now, but the map app said we were almost at the yard. I don't know what I'd been expecting, but the place which came into view was super smart. As we walked through the double gates, there was a purpose built brick yard on the left, and on the right, an outdoor school with large mirrors down the sides.

The green trailer was parked just ahead of us, ramp down, apparently drying off after having been washed out.

I rang 'woman-with-skewbald' (as I'd saved the

mother's number on my phone) and she said she'd be out in a sec. She added that if I wanted I could turn Callie out in the school.

I walked in, shut the gate, unfastened her bridle and slid it gently over her ears. Immediately she wandered off, examined the ground, pawed it experimentally, completed a full turn, then sank down gratefully into the sand. She rolled and rolled and rolled, then lurched to her feet, gave a big shake, and came to stand by me. I scratched the base of her ears, and she dropped her head and rested her nose by my hip.

'Come a long way, haven't we lass?' I murmured.

And not just geographically. Callie trusted me now. We'd built up a bit of a relationship in that walk home.

I glanced up. There in the reflection from the mirrors was the image of me with the stunningly beautiful Callie. And for the first time, it didn't seem quite so ridiculous.

The thought popped into my mind: perhaps if the girl was having problems with her... Perhaps they might be looking for a new home for Callie.

Across the yard, the mother was coming out to greet me.

I smiled back. Well, it wouldn't hurt to ask.

THE OTHER CASTLETON GIRL

The horse stood in the centre of the small, unfamiliar paddock, his head thrown up, ears pricked, nostrils flared.

Fiona crossed her arms on the top bar of the gate, rested her chin against her hand, and watched him. He was big boned, but unmuscled, so that his frame seemed ungainly under the blue roan of his coat. She saw the tension in his body, the way his black tail was held aloft like a banner behind him, and expected that any second he would bolt. Instead, he began a slow, cadenced trot following the perimeter of the paddock, as though testing out the fence line. At that moment, he looked more like a dressage horse than a show jumper.

Both Fiona's dad, Tony, and her younger sister, the great Nina Castleton, disapproved of her latest purchase. Tony, because the gelding was a six year old, with nothing much in his record of interest. They usually only bought in three and four year olds - untried, ready to bring on, cheap. Echo had been cheap enough, but only because on paper there was little to recommend him. Nina's reservations were different. In her view he was 'ugly'. 'You won't be the one riding him in public!' she had whined.

But Fiona was very taken with Echo - there was just

something about him - and since she was in charge of acquiring new stock, here he was. When she'd spotted the ad, she'd been hard pressed to feign casual interest, but she'd still got him for good money - years of haggling had taught her that. She knew he wouldn't have long to prove himself though. Horses had to earn their keep at Castleton's.

The phone in her back pocket began a subtle melodic ring. Fiona had learnt the hard way not to have anything too abrupt as a ringtone when she was schooling the youngstock. The screen said 'Dad'. She sighed.

'Alright?' came her father's terse voice.

'Fine, ta. How are you getting on?'

'She's come second in the qualifier, and she's just won with that four year old.'

'That's great, dad.'

'Nina did well - the thing has no natural balance. She had to practically hold it up over the combination.'

Fiona bit her lip. The four year old, a sweet little mare, had a super jump, but had little experience in the ring, and would have undoubtedly been nervous in her first testing competition. She'd done well to get round clear, let alone win. But of course, her dad wouldn't see it like that. All he would see was that Fiona had sent precious Nina out with a less than perfect youngster.

'So, she'll be one for the website,' Tony went on.

Which meant the mare would be up for sale. Shame. A few more months, and she might mature into something special.

'We can talk about it later,' said Fiona, diplomatically.

Her father grunted. 'How's that giraffe you bought?'

Echo had stopped at the far end of the paddock and was gazing out across the fields at the other Castleton horses he had yet to meet. He did indeed have a long neck, and long legs, and sometimes he looked a little uncoordinated when he jumped, but the description was still harsh.

'I've just turned him out for a few minutes,' said Fiona, not rising to it. 'He was cracking in the school this morning.'

'Right.' Tony's voice went muffled for a couple of seconds, and she realised he was talking to someone else. Then he came back to the phone. 'Gotta go. Speak later, yes?'

'Fine,' said Fiona. But he'd already rung off.

She pushed the phone back into her pocket and took a last glance at the horse. His muscles suddenly bunched, and he bolted back across the paddock flat out, coming to an abrupt and ragged halt in front of her, snorting. His head had the suggestion of bay colouring in the roan mix, and he had a star which merged into a thin, stuttering white stripe, ending in a snip between his flared nostrils. It was as though someone had dribbled white paint down his face, and it gave him a sweet, almost comical expression.

'You're stunning, chap,' said Fiona, reaching out and rubbing his face. 'Just let them wait.'

She always liked afternoons at the yard on a competition day - when it was just her and the horses. Sophie, their groom, had gone with Nina of course. Nina was always too busy posing and hobnobbing to do any of the mundane things like plaiting manes or tacking up. Nina the Great, as the farrier called her. And it wasn't a compliment.

But as she walked back through the stables, habitually glancing into each empty box even though she knew they were all mucked out and correct, Fiona spotted the shiny red Porsche in the yard, and her heart sank.

Spencer.

'She's not here,' Fiona called across the yard. 'It's the qualifier today.'

Spencer, propped nonchalantly against the pristine car, glanced up at her. He was wearing a casual shirt and linen trousers and his bare tanned feet were pushed into deck shoes. The whole ensemble looked effortlessly tasteful and elegant. Fiona was uncomfortably aware of her slightly soiled breeches, and the clammy feel of cooling sweat after her workout with Echo in the school. Spencer always made her feel faintly repulsive.

'S'OK.' He shrugged, reached down to the tiny back seat of the car, and withdrew an enormous bouquet of flowers. 'I'll just leave these for her.'

Fiona's skin prickled as he followed her to the office. She couldn't see what Nina saw in him - other than the money of course. Spencer - or more accurately, Spencer's father, a property mogul - had bankrolled more than one top class horse for Nina in the past.

'Just pop them on the desk.' Fiona pasted on her best smile. 'I'll see she gets them tonight.'

'Thanks.'

He stood gazing at the photographs on the wall - Nina jumping at Horse of the Year Show, at several county shows, at Hickstead. Pictures he'd seen a thousand times before.

Why didn't he just go?

'Um...' He pushed one hand through his hair, and then turned towards her, not quite meeting her eye. 'I wanted to ask you a favour actually.'

Fiona couldn't have been more surprised if he'd announced he wanted to be a unicorn. When Nina was around, Spencer would hardly acknowledge Fiona. The thought that he needed her help with something was incredible.

'O*kay*.' She knew her voice sounded wary.

He grinned suddenly, and shook his head, as though he too was finding it hard to credit. 'You're going to think this is a bit mad. And, I mean, say 'no' if you want. And obviously, don't say anything to Nina.'

Oh my God, he's going to ask me out, thought Fiona suddenly.

'I want to do something to really prove to Nina how I

feel about her,' said Spencer, 'something that will really impress her.'

Ha! Read that wrong, Fiona thought with a curious mix of relief and disappointment. It would have been fun to have turned him down, outraged.

'O*kay*,' she repeated. 'Are you looking for suggestions?'

'Erm, no. I've had an idea.'

'Right. Good.' There was another interminable pause. Fiona wanted to strangle him. 'So..... where do I come in?'

'I'd like to learn to ride. I was hoping you'd give me a few lessons.'

Fiona's heart sank into her boots.

'Wouldn't you be better off at a proper riding school?' she said carefully. 'I mean, we've not got much here to train a novice on.'

'Well, yes - I appreciate that. But... I *know* you. And I want to be able to ride horses like these.' He gestured towards the stables, even though they were currently empty. 'Not some riding school dobbin.'

Fiona blew out her cheeks. 'Couldn't you get Nina to teach you? Be fun, learning with her wouldn't it?'

'I want it to be a surprise.'

Spencer met her eye for the first time. He didn't look like the usual smooth, over-confident Spencer. His expression could only be described as earnest.

Fiona gave a helpless shrug. 'OK. Why not?' She could think of a million reasons why not, but she was bad at letting people down. 'It'll have to be when Nina's out, of course. Give me your number and I'll text you.'

They swapped numbers; Fiona felt strangely uncomfortable even though it was for a genuine reason.

He headed for the door. 'Have you got something to wear?' she asked, looking meaningfully at his linen trousers.

'I'll get kitted out, don't worry.' He grinned at her. 'Thanks for this - appreciate it.'

Fiona watched him walk back to the car, and then sank

down in the office chair. What on earth had she got herself into?

Fiona was in Echo's box when the lorry returned. The horse darted to the door and stuck his head out as far as his long neck would let him. Fiona, hand on his shoulder to remind him she was there, leaned over the door beside him and watched Nina slide down from the passenger door of the cab. Still in her show breeches, and a slim fitting shirt, she looked as elegant as it was possible to be after a whole day travelling and competing. Fiona wondered, not for the first time, if she and Nina were genuinely the product of the same parental genes. Perhaps there simply wasn't a gene for poise?

Sophie was already unloading the two horses, while Nina was messing with her phone. Fiona let herself out of Echo's box, gave him a final pat, and went across to the office. She kept meticulous records of all the horses' achievements and would have to note down the day's results.

The flowers lay on the desk. Spencer. Oh God! She scooped up the bouquet, and carried it out. Nina eyes widened. 'The darling! But what a dafty - he knew I was away today. Must have forgotten!' She whipped out her phone straightaway. 'Spencer, you silly!'

'When's he going to pop the question, that's what I want to know?' Toby was rubbing his knee and kneading the muscle of his left thigh. He looked exhausted. His eyes were red rimmed, and his face ashen. He was finding the driving harder nowadays. Another role Fiona was trying to avoid taking on.

'Go on in, dad. I'll sort the lorry.'

'I'm alright.'

'You're not though, are you?'

He waved her away, and limped off towards the house.

Sophie had the two horses in their boxes by now, and was settling them for the night. Fiona mucked out the lorry, fetched out the tack and equipment, then hoisted herself into the cab. Nina's rosettes were strewn across the dashboard. Fiona picked up the red one, won by the little four year old mare, and ran her fingertips across the ribbon. When they'd been kids it was just the same. Nina had won fistfuls of the things. For Fiona, always paralysed by fear in competitions, always taking the wrong course, or having an unlucky stop because she didn't have the courage of her convictions, the few rosettes she ever won were precious beyond belief. They were still pinned, faded and dusty, to a board in her bedroom. Pathetic really, when Nina's collection could have filled every wall in their lounge.

She tossed the rosette back on the dashboard, and started the engine.

It didn't matter. People were good at different things. Nina was the competition rider, but Fiona schooled the horses at home - gave the youngsters the best start she could. She had the patience, she kept calm when an inexperienced horse threw a tantrum in the arena. She made the horses which Nina went on to ride to fame. As long as she never had to enter a competition herself, it was fine.

She backed the lorry slowly and carefully into the space at the back of the barn, inching in between the tractor and the barn's corrugated roof.

Oh yeah, and she was a better driver than Nina too!

It had been worth getting up at the crack of dawn. With the yard quiet, Echo had settled straight away and was working beautifully over a grid of small fences. He listened to her as she asked him to go again, this time off a shorter stride, and again, this time lengthening. Fiona brought him back to a trot and worked on some circles, getting him to flex. Then she brought him back to a walk, let him have a long rein, and enjoyed his enormous powerful stride moving fluidly beneath her.

'Lovely!'

Fiona glanced round. Sophie was in the walk-way with a coffee in her hand. With her free hand, she gave Fiona a thumbs up.

Echo noticed her inattention, or maybe it was the strange person watching. His head came up, and the fluidity was replaced by tension.

'OK, lad,' said Fiona, putting her hand on his neck.

Sophie turned away and headed towards the stables. The horse watched her go, flicked an ear back at Fiona, and then seemed to let out a breath.

Funny old thing, thought Fiona. She was glad Sophie had seen them working. It was nice to have an ally.

She walked Echo until he cooled, then kicked her feet out of the stirrups and slid to the floor. Her moment to herself was over. There was still all the mucking out do, then a quick bite of breakfast before schooling the other youngsters.

She finished three boxes before she had to give in to her hunger. She paused as she always did to ask Sophie if she wanted anything. It was a little ritual. Sophie, who seemed to live on coffee alone and was stick thin, always said no. Just once or twice in the depths of winter had she been persuaded to thaw out in the kitchen for a few minutes. Still, Fiona liked to check.

The kitchen smelled of burnt toast. Fiona pulled off her boots and padded across the tiles leaving a trail of hay bits.

Nina was standing by the worktop with an intense look of concentration on her face. Her hair was twisted up in a clip, and a couple of small tendrils had come loose, framing her face. She was in the process of gluing a false nail back on.

'Not helping with the mucking out this morning then?' asked Fiona dryly.

'Got that YouTube woman coming, haven't I?' Nina

muttered, not looking up.

'Oh yes, your *interview.*' Fiona put the words in air quotes, and grinned.

'She's got well over 100,000 subscribers,' said Nina. 'About four times as many people as buy that.' She nodded at the copy of the equestrian magazine that was lying on the kitchen table. 'This kind of exposure will help put us on the map, and might even help sell a nag or two, eh?' She shoved the box of false nails into a drawer, flashed Fiona a mirthless smile, and headed towards the door. At the last minute she paused, turned and looked at Fiona meaningfully. 'I'd get changed, if I were you - I doubt they'll actually want to talk to you, but chances are you'll be in shot at some point and you look a state.'

'You'd look a state if you lifted one of those manicured fingers to do any actual work!' Fiona shouted after her. But Nina was gone.

Fiona sighed. Sometimes she would start the day determined not to have a row with her sister, and yet moments into their first conversation, they would find themselves goading each other. It wasn't like they hated each other - far from it - but there was always an undercurrent. We're too different, thought Fiona. We care about different stuff.

Take the YouTube thing. Fiona thought it was pointless, ego-massaging trash. She wasn't a luddite - she managed the website and the accounts software - but she trusted spreadsheets and calculations, not videos that went viral or social media influencers that had a zillion followers.

Which is one of the many reasons Nina is ideal sponsorship material and I am not, thought Fiona. She glanced down at herself. Nina had a point - she did look pretty awful. Echo's saddle had left brown tide marks on her breeches, and there was hay and shavings stuck to her fleece jacket. She went gloomily upstairs to change. It seemed ridiculous when she was just going to carry on mucking out.

'What's that bloke up to?'

Tony stood gazing across the yard at the jump paddock.

Fiona lay down her shavings fork and went to stand by her father. 'It's the cameraman.'

'The what?'

'He's with the YouTube woman.'

'Well, what's he doing?'

'Cameraman stuff - I don't know. He's probably looking for the best angle or measuring the light or something.'

'Snooping, that's what. I'll sort him!'

Fiona lay a restraining hand on his arm. The cameraman stepped backwards a couple of paces, filming Nina walking up from the paddocks with the interviewer.

'Bloody rubbish,' said Tony.

'Nina's confident it'll be good publicity for us,' said Fiona. 'Apparently this woman's got a big following.'

'She's got a big arse, I know that much,' said Tony sourly. 'Getting some horses ready for competition would be a better way of getting us some publicity!'

'That's my job!' said Fiona.

'Hmm. How's the giraffe?'

'Rode him this morning - went really well.'

'Good. Sooner he improves, the sooner we can get shot of him.'

'You won't want to get rid of him in a few weeks,' said Fiona. 'Trust me.'

Tony laughed. 'I'd trust you with anything except horses - you're too soft, that's your problem. Fall in love with them all. If you had your way, we'd have fields full of pets.'

Fiona smiled and let it pass.

Echo was a star in the making. She knew it. And one day, so would her father.

It was 9.30pm by the time Fiona flopped down on the sofa in the lounge. The TV was on, but neither Tony nor Nina was watching. Tony had fallen asleep, and Nina was on her phone, feet tucked up under her in the big armchair. Fiona stared for a couple of minutes at the crime drama on the screen, but she'd missed too much to be able to work out what was going on, and none of the characters grabbed her. She knew she should go to bed; she was knackered and a decent night's sleep would do wonders, but she found herself as reluctant as a child. It was only 9.30pm! She'd had no evening - no time to herself yet.

Her phone buzzed with a message.

Spencer! Oh God, she'd forgotten about him. The weight of her promise weighed her down. Why did he want to learn to ride? And why on earth had she agreed to teach him? She opened the message with a mixture of irritation and guilt.

- Hey Fi, Nina said Tony was taking her to jump at Sedgeworth on Weds. How about I come over when they've gone - just let me know what time?

Fiona bristled. For one, he'd never called her Fi to her face (in fact, he never used her name at all, come to think of it) so it sounded oddly familiar in a text. And for another, the text itself felt pestering. She's only agreed to this the previous day. Bloody men, she thought. Bloody privileged men!

She'd never had time for boyfriends. That's what she told herself (and what she'd told one or two guys too). The last man in her life was Andy, a local lad who, when he couldn't bear working alongside his father on the farm, started his own paddock maintenance business. He still came over every now and then, when they needed the hedges cutting back, or a field topped, and he and Fiona were still friendly, if not friends. But there was precious little opportunity for romance in this game, and to be honest, she wasn't even aware of missing it.

'When are you jumping next?' she asked Nina.

Without looking up, Nina said, 'Wednesday. Sedgeworth. Why?'

'I'm trying to sync my calendar on my phone,' lied Fiona. 'I had a feeling it was Wednesday, but it wasn't coming up,'

Nina rolled her eyes. 'You and your spreadsheets and calendars! I just *know*.'

'Like you just *know* what each of your horses has for breakfast - oh no wait, you don't - because you don't get your arse out of bed in time to feed them.'

'Yeah, well we employ someone to do that, but you're such a control freak that you don't trust her to get on with her job.'

Fiona opened her mouth to make another retort, but stopped herself. She'd resolved not to row with her sister. She would let it pass.

She texted Spencer back:

- Just checked. Yes, that's fine as Sophie will go with them. Will let you know what time.

She pushed herself to her feet. 'Right, I'm going up. This control freak has to get her beauty sleep.'

'Ha!' said Nina, 'there's -'

' - not enough hours in the night!' Fiona finished for her. 'Yeah, I know.' She glanced at Tony. 'Try to make him go up soon, eh? Doesn't do him any good falling asleep down here.'

Nina made a face. 'It's those tablets he takes for his knee - they knock him out.'

'Hmm. We've got to remember, he's not getting any younger.'

'Don't let him hear you say that!' said Nina.

The two girls grinned at each other - a momentary truce.

'You weren't kidding, were you?'

Spencer glanced down at himself. 'What?'

'You look like you've just stepped from the page of a

magazine.'

Spencer made a face. 'All the gear...'

'I'd worry about the boots,' said Fiona, gazing at them critically.

'Why? What's wrong with them?'

'Nothing. They're beautiful.' She tried to keep the covetous note out of her voice. 'But they're brand new. The leather will be a bit stiff to start with. Look, go and stand on the bottom step of the mounting block.'

She watched him step up, looking even more like a model now.

'Stand with your toes on the edge - other way - and drop your heels. Lower. Lower. See - too stiff. You'll have to practise at home.'

'If you say so.' He stepped down. 'So, who am I riding?'

'Boris,' said Fiona, leading them towards the big bay who was standing tacked up ready in the cross ties.

'He's huge,' said Spencer. 'Haven't you got something smaller? Not so far to fall?'

'You're not going to fall. Besides, Boris is the safest thing we've got. He's the most experienced. If you wobble, he'll most likely stop to let you sort yourself out.'

'If you're sure,' said Spencer, doubtfully.

'You're the one who wanted to do this,' Fiona reminded him.

'I'm rather forgetting why!' Spencer looked slightly green.

'Think of Nina. Think how touched she'll feel that you've done this for her.'

Spencer grinned. 'You're, absolutely right - thank you. I want to make Nina proud.' He took a breath. 'OK, let's do it!'

It was safe to say Spencer was not a natural. Fiona didn't think she had ever seen anyone look quite so uncomfortable on a horse. His upper body was too far forward and curled as though he was trying to protect his stomach from imminent attack. His legs were clinging to Boris's sides; knees pressed into the saddle, so that his feet were constantly slipping out of the irons. His hands were awful. Fiona had tried to use the analogy of holding two cups of tea to stop him turning them horizontally, but this had the effect of making him appear to hold them rigid over Boris's withers. Coupled with the poor upper body posture, and the look of intense concentration on his face, he looked rather like an ageing butler determined not to drop a couple of priceless decanters.

Poor Boris walked at half speed around the school with his ears back, casting a worried eye in Fiona's direction as if he was saying, 'Erm....really?'

Fiona bit her lip trying not to laugh. And then the enormity of what she'd taken on struck her. She'd never actually taught anyone to ride, not from scratch. Nor could she remember being taught to ride. They had just ridden. Fiona had a dim recollection of her mum walking around with her on the lead rein, but she couldn't be sure if that was a real memory, or something she'd made up from looking at old photographs. Nina sometimes gave lessons, to aspiring youngsters whose parents wanted them to be just like Nina - but again, all these kids could ride already - they came to Nina to glean the finer points of show jumping, or just to be able to say, 'My trainer? Oh yes, I go to Nina Castleton.'

Fiona, out of the limelight, did not gain the same following - nor had she any wish to acquire one. She was happy to stick to training horses. This with Spencer would be very much a one off.

'OK, remember what I said to you about using your weight and seat and legs to tell him to stop - not just pulling on the reins. Almost like you're just thinking "stop" - OK?'

'I *am* thinking "stop"!' said Spencer. 'But to be honest, I've been thinking "stop" since we started so he probably can't tell.'

Fiona started to giggle.

'That's not helpful,' said Spencer.

'OK, gently introduce some resistance on the reins. Don't pull, just stop going with him.'

Boris came to an awkward halt with his head in the air and one hind leg stuck out to the side.

'I did it!' said Spencer. 'Oh, good lad!' He patted Boris enthusiastically.

Boris yanked the reins out of Spencer's hands so he could lower his head.

'Well done!' said Fiona, walking over and giving Boris an appreciative head rub. 'So now we have to work on the subtlety of your aids.'

Fiona stood at Boris's head while Spencer slid to the floor.

'Oh my God, how long was that?' he said, involuntarily stepping back, his legs apparently refusing to work properly. 'Must have been an hour?'

Fiona looked at her watch. 'Thirty two minutes.'

Spencer groaned. 'I'll never walk again.'

'Wait until you try to learn the rising trot,' said Fiona, darkly.

'Why? What happens then?'

'Well, let's just say Nina won't thank you if your horse riding puts you out of action, so to speak.' Fiona tapped the pommel of the saddle to illustrate her point.

'Ah.'

They walked slowly back to the yard with Boris between them. Fiona was thankful the first lesson was over. Hopefully Spencer would be so crippled by the time he woke up the following day that it would also be the last.

'Thanks so much for this,' said Spencer, watching Fiona untack Boris and rest his saddle on the stable door.

'No problem.'

'Hope you don't think I'm too hopeless to be taught.'

'Course not,' Fiona lied. She flicked a brush quickly

over the saddle marks - not that Boris had worked up a sweat during his half hour in walk!

'We never discussed your fee.'

'Oh, don't be silly.'

'I don't expect you to give up your time for nothing,' said Spencer. 'If you tell me your rate, and I'll transfer the money.'

Fiona shook her head. 'You're my sister's partner - you're practically family - I'm not going to charge you.'

'That's very kind.' Spencer looked uncomfortable. 'Are you sure?'

Fiona grinned at him. 'We both know that once anyone gets to "Are you sure?" the discussion is settled.'

'That's very true. Never thought of it like that before.' Spencer dipped his head to concede the point. 'Thank you, Fi.'

Fi. Funny, this time it didn't seem so irritating.

On Friday, a shy girl came with her father to try the little four year old mare. Fiona watched with a mixture of pride and sadness as first Nina, and then the girl, rode the mare in the outdoor school. She behaved perfectly both on the flat, and around the course of fences. The girl had a nice seat and rode sympathetically and, given the mare *had* to go, Fiona hoped she would end up going to this nice shy lass rather than someone more bullish.

She left the prospective purchasers with her father to haggle over the sale price, while she took the mare back to her box. They would need to sort out a date for the vetting. The mare watched her with gentle brown eyes.

'You don't know you're going, do you, sweetie?' said Fiona rubbing her behind the ears. 'I'll miss you round the yard. You're so easy, such a nice little lady.'

The mare nudged her with her nose.

It was always like this. Fiona hated to see them go. Maybe her dad was right - maybe she was too soft.

Nina appeared. 'Looks like they're having her.' She

gave the mare a pat. 'She's a nice little thing, isn't she?'

'Just not nice enough, eh?' said Fiona feelingly.

'Well, she's never going to be world class,' said Nina. Her phone buzzed, and she pulled it out of her pocket. 'Spencer.' She made the daft face she always did when it was Spencer.

'Ask him -' Fiona began, and stopped herself. She'd been meaning to say, 'Ask him if he's still stiff' but of course she couldn't say why.

Nina looked at her curiously.

'- if he's got any more flowers for you!' she finished lamely.

'You're just jealous because you never get bought flowers!' said Nina, and she flounced off.

Oops! thought Fiona, grinning to herself. That was close!

Fiona had lost some time with the prospective purchasers, meaning she was behind schedule in working the youngsters. By six she'd caught up with everyone bar the six year old chestnut gelding, Soldier's Gold (Rusty) that both Tony and Nina were keen on as their star of the future. On the training schedule, he was supposed to hack that day and jump the following day, but since the jumps were still up in the outdoor, she decided to swap his sessions round.

The sun was beginning to dip behind the trees, but it was pleasant enough warming up. She did some work on either rein, and although Rusty wasn't particularly enthusiastic to start with, he soon settled. She popped an inviting cross a couple of times, working on maintaining the rhythm, and then practised turning each direction from landing. He wasn't quite as happy on the right rein, she noticed. Finally, she took him on round to an oxer, then onto a single bar with a filler, then a related distance across the school, a change of rein and a wall, and then the only really challenging fence - a triple bar - to finish.

As she pulled up and patted Rusty, she heard clapping behind her. She turned. Spencer was standing by the fence. She rode over self-consciously.

'Nina's in the house getting ready,' she said, walking Rusty in small slow circles to cool down. 'Off somewhere nice?'

'Going for a bite to eat.' He nodded at Rusty. 'That was pretty impressive.'

'Just a schooling round, nothing major,' said Fiona with a shrug.

Spencer shook his head with a grin. He looked as though he was going to say something else, but at that moment Nina appeared from the house, called and waved. Spencer said, 'I'll leave you to it then. Goodnight.'

Fiona turned Rusty and did another lap of the school in walk, watching Nina and Spencer climbing into the Porsche. Did she envy them? Would she rather be at this very second speeding towards a nice little bistro somewhere in a fancy car? Rusty shook his head, and his mane tumbled either side of his neck for a moment, in a rich fiery wave. She grinned. Nope. Quite happy where she was.

As it turned out, lesson two didn't take place until a week later when Nina and Tony had gone off to discuss a potential sponsorship deal with a local clothing company. Apparently the slim, blonde and beautiful Nina was just the kind of rider they were looking for to endorse their products.

'If she gets this deal, she'll become even more insufferable!' said Fiona to Sophie as they watched Nina lowering herself into the passenger seat of the car, looking even more impossibly elegant than usual.

Sophie shook her head. 'I don't know how she does it. The other week, we were at a show, and it absolutely tipped down between classes. The rest of us looked like drowned rats. Nina? No, the rain made her hair fall into dainty ringlets, and there were these little drops of water on her jacket that looked like bloody diamonds!'

Fiona sniggered. 'And we look like this!' she said, looking down at herself and Sophie.

'Uh-huh!' Sophie picked up her coat. 'Which is why I'm off for a shower! See you tomorrow.'

'Yes, have a good afternoon.'

Fiona waited for Sophie's car to go before she texted Spencer the all-clear.

'Hang on - was I that bad last time you're putting me on the lead rein?' asked Spencer when Fiona produced the lunge line.

'This is so you can forget about starting and stopping and steering, and concentrate on how it feels to be in the saddle.'

'Okay.' Spencer sounded dubious.

'You wanted to learn to ride,' said Fiona. 'This wasn't my idea. If you don't want to do this, I've got plenty of other things I could be doing.'

Spencer held up a hand. 'I'm sure you have. Look, sorry - I'm really grateful for you taking the time to do this. And I *do* want to learn. But I am pretty nervous too.' He gave a lopsided grin. 'You guys, you've done this all your lives - you make it look so easy. I get on, and all I can think of is how much it'll hurt when I come off.'

'So, don't do it. No-one is making you.'

'That's rather the point.' Spencer went to push his hands through his hair, and instead his fingertips hit his riding hat. He dropped his hand helplessly. 'My father is always berating me for being directionless, for not having any backbone. He says I'm a born follower, not a leader. Thinks I run away from every challenge. This one I need to face.'

Fiona was momentarily disarmed. Spencer had always seemed cavalier in his attitude to everything. As though nothing much mattered to him. As though there were no consequences to anything. This level of self-analysis was alien. She didn't know what to say.

'Oh, and I know that everything I've just said is neither cool nor manly, so when I finally reveal to Nina with a flourish that I can ride - assuming of course I ever get to that stage - well, I'd be really grateful if you didn't mention what a big coward I was to begin with.'

'It's not cowardly to do something when you're scared - quite the reverse,' said Fiona. 'And if it makes you feel better, I'm a coward.'

'Not where riding is concerned.'

'Oh yes I am.'

'Rubbish. I saw you the other night - jumping those enormous fences out there.' He waved a hand in the direction of the outdoor school.

'Yup. And that's the only place you'll see me jump. Here, at home. Safe in the knowledge that no-one's watching.'

'I was watching.'

'Yes, but at the time I didn't know that.' Fiona took a breath. 'It's always been like it for me. At home, I can jump anything. When we were kids we'd take our ponies round and round, jumping higher and higher - until mum came and told us off of course!' She grinned at the memory. 'But on show days, I'd be sick in the mornings - physically sick. And on the journey, I'd feel desperately cold, even on a beautiful day. When we'd get to the show ground, I'd hardly be able to get out of the car. Dad thought I was being lazy and would shout at me to get a move on. Because Nina was younger, her classes were usually before mine - sometimes we'd be in the same one - but she'd usually ride before me and be brilliant. When it came to my turn, I'd ride into the ring, and my legs - you know people say 'like jelly' - well, yes, exactly that. I couldn't make them work. And I'd ride towards the first fence, and my poor pony would wonder what the hell was going on. He'd maybe pop the first couple of fences to be obliging, but as soon as we reached anything tricky, I'd usually start having refusals and get eliminated. And that would be that. Nina would go home with a fistful of rosettes and I'd...well...I'd gaze at her rosettes and... You get the picture.'

Spencer seemed momentarily stunned. 'Why did your parents keep taking you if you didn't want to go?'

'But I did want to go, that was just it. When we put the entries in, I *wanted* to do it. And I'd practise at home. And I knew we *could* do it. It was just on the day it would always fall apart.'

'But you kept trying?'

'I stopped competing when I was about 13. Couldn't bear the kids from school taking the piss. And besides, about that time dad bought a three year old to bring on, and I started helping him, and then I decided that's what I wanted to do. Nina wasn't interested in all that. She just wanted to jump and win more rosettes and trophies. So that's what happened. I started backing and bringing on the youngsters - she kept jumping. And, as you know, that's what we're still doing.'

'Wow.' Spencer looked at her curiously.

'I suppose I assumed Nina had told you all that,' said Fiona. 'But maybe it never came up.'

'She just said you weren't interested in competing.'

Fiona shrugged. 'Well, that's kind of true. I guess we all have to be realistic about what we're like as people. Nina loves it - the adrenaline rush, the people watching, being the centre of attention. But it's not for me.'

Spencer shook his head slowly, then looked at her. 'Right, well, that's put my nerves into perspective.' He stood on the mounting block and picked up Boris's reins. 'Let's do this!'

After Spencer had gone, Fiona put Echo in the cross ties and started grooming. He was filling out and muscling up, so he no longer looked quite so ungainly. His roan coat shone with health and he stood calmly while Fiona fetched his tack. As she worked, she thought about Spencer - about their conversation. Why had she told him all that stuff about her childhood? She wanted to take it all back - protect her privacy. She'd never told anyone about how she'd really felt on show days - except her mum, of course.

But it had been easy to talk to Spencer. She wasn't quite sure why. There was something about him, calm, non-judgemental. She thought of what he'd said about his father - making him feel as though he somehow wasn't man enough. Parents, eh?

She led Echo out to the outdoor school, climbed aboard from the mounting block and tightened her girths. There was a stiff breeze, rustling the leaves in the trees. The rugs in the racks outside each stable shivered and their buckles clinked. Echo's ears flicked. She started him off on a loose rein, felt him start at the least thing, but she kept focused, and gradually, he started to settle - his ears flicking back to her, waiting for her instructions. They worked together for 20 mins on the flat, riding between the fences, until they were totally in sync, and then she brought him into the first schooling fence. He popped it like it was nothing, ears pricked, looking for the next thing. She turned him towards a low spread with a cross in front, then on to an oxer. His stride was even and he took her strongly into the fences without rushing. She asked him to shorten slightly, so that the power was contained in his haunches, and then sent him to the triple bar. It was a glorious feeling. She couldn't keep the grin off her face. She bloody loved this horse.

Nina could not object to riding him now.

The following morning, Nina came bouncing into the kitchen, waving a letter. 'Formal agreement for the sponsorship deal!'

'You got it?' Fiona took the proffered letter and skim read the details. 'Blimey, you're doing a photo shoot!'

'Uh-huh. And I get a whole wardrobe for both me and the horses. And they're going to pay to re-do the livery on the lorry. It'll be this really classy grey with a thin line of burgundy-red.'

'And best of all, a big cheque!' Fiona's eyes widened at the figure.

'See - it pays to put yourself out there,' said Nina. 'Guess how they found out about me?'

Fiona handed back the letter. 'Go on?'

'The Managing Director's daughter saw me on YouTube!' And with that, Nina stuck her tongue out at Fiona as though she was about eight, and flounced out of the room.

'Christ!' Tony gazed at the horse and rider in the school with a look of disbelief.

Nina, who usually looked perfect on any horse, was not having a good ride. For one thing, Echo, tall and rangy, seemed out of proportion with her own slight frame. For another, he clearly wasn't taking any notice of her.

Fiona bit her lip. She didn't understand it. The last three times she'd ridden him, she would have said Echo was the most promising youngster she'd ever sat on. He'd worked beautifully for her. And whatever their feelings of rivalry, she knew her sister could ride, so it wasn't that Echo was taking the mickey out of her. Rather, Echo looked completely terrified - as though he'd never been in the school before.

'Have you done *anything* with him?' asked Tony.

'Yes, I told you, he's been working beautifully,' Fiona protested.

They watched Echo leap sideways at a leaf, and then refuse to go into the far corner of the school, giving a mini-rear when Nina tried to force him on with her legs.

'I've never seen him like this,' said Fiona.

Nina had turned him and was riding back towards them. She kicked her feet out of the irons and slithered to the floor. 'You ride him!' she said, holding out the reins to Fiona.

Fiona sighed and went to fetch her hat. When she took the reins from Nina, Echo spun in a circle. Nina managed to leg her into the saddle, but he jogged away before Fiona could slip her feet into the stirrups.

'Hey, the lad - what's up,' she said to him. 'Steady, the boy.'

His ears flicked. But his head was in the air, his back hollow.

Fiona focused on him entirely, keeping her legs wrapped softly around his body, keeping the contact with the rein even. She talked to him constantly, kept him moving forward, kept changing the rein, giving him something to think about. Time faded away. She did not think about the critical gazes of Tony and Nina. There was just Echo. He began to settle, to concentrate. Fiona kept him working like she did in all their schooling sessions. Eventually she started to jump. His jumping was as good as ever, but she noticed his slight hesitation going towards the wall. It's not the fence, she thought, it's because he's distracted by Nina and Tony in his eye line.

She remembered that time in the indoor school when Sophie had come to watch.

Of course.

She pushed him on around the school, turned a circle so he had to pass the bystanders again and again, and then on and around the school, changing the rein and doing the same on the other rein. She took him over all the jumps again, and he was foot-perfect. She pulled up, let him walk at the far end. He gave a long snort, and she felt all the tension go out of him.

'I know how you feel, chap,' she said, giving him a pat. 'I know how you feel.'

When she rode back to Tony and Nina, Tony said, 'Pop him on the website. He looks good enough. Let's not waste any more time on him.'

Fiona stared at him. 'You are kidding?'

'Why?' Tony frowned.

'Did you not see how well he just went?'

'Yeah, well, you've proved he goes fine for you but that's no bloody good, is it? He's got to go well for Nina.'

'And he will - he just needs more time to get used to her.'

Nina shook her head. 'You *know*, don't you - you just know when you don't gel with a horse. He's not for me. Sorry Fi - I know you think a lot of him.'

'I'm not selling him,' said Fiona. 'He's the best horse we've ever had here.'

Tony made a noise of derision. 'So, are you going to ride him then?'

Fiona glared at him. 'If that's what it takes.'

Tony and Nina stared at her.

'You're going to jump him?' Nina asked incredulously.

'Don't make it sound like I've just proposed flying to the moon!' Fiona snapped. 'I can ride, you know.'

And she rode off to the bottom of the school. Her heart was thudding in her chest, the sweat cooling down her spine.

What had she just promised to do?

Fiona watched critically as Spencer and Boris executed a 20 metre circle in trot. Spencer was rising a little too obviously, and Boris wasn't really carrying himself with quite as much aplomb as he could do if, say, Nina was riding him, but to be honest they didn't look too bad.

'OK, back to walk, and again on the other rein.'

Spencer obediently changed the rein and set off to the left. There was a moment where he bumped in the saddle and then he got into the rhythm of Boris's stride. He completed the circle, then came back to walk.

'Perfect, give him a pat and a long rein,' said Fiona. 'That'll do for today. I think you've cracked it.'

Spencer beamed. 'Really? I mean, it felt pretty good.

But it looked OK too?'

'Yes, honestly - don't sound so surprised!' Fiona grinned. She watched him walk Boris for a few minutes and had to admit, if you didn't know, you would assume watching the way he let Boris have his head and stretch down, and how easily he now sat in the saddle, that Spencer could ride.

'We'll try a canter next time,' she said as Spencer rode over to her.

'That would be brilliant.' He grinned. 'Listen to me sounding so enthusiastic! A few weeks ago I would have been thinking you wanted to get me killed!'

Fiona rubbed Boris's nose affectionately. 'He's taught you well.'

'No, you've taught me well.' Spencer slid to the ground beside her. 'I don't know how to thank you.'

Before she could reply, Fiona's stomach rumbled loudly.

Spencer looked at her meaningfully. 'Could I perhaps take you for a late lunch?'

Fiona shook her head with a grin. 'No, I'm fine. I've got to sort him out,' she said indicating Boris. 'And then I've got another one to ride, and some tack to clean.'

'But you're going to eat?'

'Yeah, I'll grab something.' Fiona started to run up Boris's stirrups and took his reins over his head to lead him back to the stables.

'I didn't want to say anything - one should never comment on a lady's weight, after all - and I hope you won't mind me mentioning it, but you do look like you could do with a good meal.'

'I've just been really busy recently,' said Fiona.

'Too busy to eat?'

'Just busy.'

They headed towards the stables.

'It's nothing to do with what Nina told me the other day, is it?'

'Why - what did Nina tell you?' Fiona put Boris in the cross ties, and pulled his saddle off.

'About you jumping Echo.'

'Oh, that.'

'Yes, that. I thought you said you didn't compete anymore.'

Fiona put down the brush she was holding and leaned against Boris's solid shoulder. She shut her eyes. 'I know. But if I don't ride him, he'll have to be sold. And I don't want to sell him.'

'That's understandable. But do you think you can do it?'

Fiona looked at the floor. 'I don't know.'

Spencer put his hand on her shoulder. She looked up. 'If it helps,' he said, 'I think you can.'

She couldn't speak. She was suddenly on the verge of tears.

'I think you can do anything you put your mind to,' Spencer went on, taking his hand away, and putting it on his own chest. 'After all, you made me - me! - into someone who could pass for a rider!'

He pulled a silly face, and in spite of everything, she found herself smiling.

'Well.... *ish*,' she said.

'Hey! You said I looked alright!' he protested.

They grinned at each other.

For the first time Fiona noticed the light in his eyes when he was smiling.

'Right, I'd better get on,' she said, picking up the brush, and untying Boris.

'Of course.' Spencer stood back. 'You're sure about lunch?'

'Yes, really. But thanks for the offer.'

'I'll leave it as an open invitation then,' he said.

She led Boris out to the top paddock and turned him out. By the time she had turned and walked back to the yard, the Porsche was just pulling out of the drive.

When he was gone, she took a deep breath and let it out slowly.

Fiona looked at herself critically in the wardrobe mirror. She didn't own an extensive range of 'going out' clothes - mainly because she never went out. The understated black trousers and the pretty blouse with the little embroidered flowers were her go-to outfit of choice. But tonight they looked all wrong. Not only were the trousers strangely saggy, but the blouse looked not so much pretty as frumpy.

Bloody Spencer. Why had he felt the need to take them all out? Why not just take Nina to celebrate the new sponsorship deal? Then she could have looked forward to spending the evening in, slobbing in front of the telly, not standing here panicking about what to bloody wear.

Another thought flashed through her mind. *You're not middle aged - you shouldn't be in every night.*

And, more disturbingly: *you're secretly excited you're going out in Spencer's company - otherwise you wouldn't be stressing about what to wear.*

In exasperation, she yanked open the wardrobe door and started dragging the coat-hangers screeching along the rail. Wedged up against the far left side of the wardrobe was a quality but very dated wool coat. She lifted out the hanger. The coat was black, three quarter length, with chunky buttons. She couldn't remember ever having worn it. Possibly an old one of her mum's? She held up a sleeve and the coat opened out. Underneath the coat was a little black dress. Fiona freed the dress from the coat hanger and examined it. Some kind of slightly stretchy material, shot through with threads of silver. She dimly remembered borrowing it years ago - a useful, non-crumble garment to throw in a bag when travelling to shows with Nina back in the day, just in case they went out somewhere. *Just in case!* Not that she ever had.

On impulse, she pulled off the saggy trousers and

frumpy blouse and pulled on the dress. The fabric fitted against her body, felt snug and sexy. She fumbled for some shoes. Again, not much choice, but one old pair of black heels.

She did not recognise herself.

For a moment she hesitated - she didn't have the nerve to wear this. Tony would take the mick. Nina would think - well, actually, she didn't know what Nina would think.

Then she glanced at her watch. There was no time to find anything else. It would have to do.

'Bloody hell! Legs!' said Tony, when she walked into the kitchen. 'Haven't seen them for years!'

Nina was putting on her shoes, resting a hand on Spencer's arm for balance. They both stared at her.

'Shut up, dad - she looks great,' said Nina. She glanced up at Spencer. 'Doesn't she?'

Spencer was still staring. He opened his mouth to reply but at that moment, the back door flew open and Sophie stumbled in backwards, kicking off her wellies.

'Sorry I'm late folks - the equine babysitter is here!'

'Thanks so much for coming back over,' said Fiona, grateful for the distraction. 'The evening feeds are on the chart. A few of the youngsters are out anyway, so you won't need to worry about them. I've made an adjustment to a couple of supplements which need to go in some of the feeds.'

'It's fine - I'll work it all out.' Sophie grinned. 'Go and have fun.'

'There's loads of human food in too if *you* need feeding,' said Nina, rolling her eyes. 'Help yourself to whatever.'

Spencer put his arm around Nina and said, 'Well, if we're all ready? We should probably go.'

They trooped outside, Fiona tottering in her unaccustomed heels. Instead of the classic Porsche, there was a sleek, black Mercedes parked on the drive.

'Borrowed from my dad,' said Spencer.

'Does he know?' asked Nina with a giggle.

'Of course!'

Nina got in the passenger side and pulled the seat forward so Tony had plenty of leg room for his dodgy knee. Fiona slipped in behind Spencer. It was like being in some kind of bizarre dream, wearing the unfamiliar dress, and sitting in this opulent car. She fumbled for the seat belt, clicked herself in, and when she glanced up, she caught Spencer's eye in the rear view mirror.

'Comfortable in the back?' he asked.

She nodded.

'Smashing!' said Tony.

It wasn't a long journey. Tony and Spencer discussed the merits of the Mercedes, with more male bravado than knowledge of the facts, and after a while Fiona tuned out. She imagined being in the passenger seat, sitting alongside Spencer as he drove. Imagined what it would feel like if it was just the two of them. She would of course have known what it felt like if she'd accepted his lunch offer the other day.

Why hadn't she said yes to lunch?

Because she'd been busy, because it would have been too much of a faff to get changed, because she wasn't good at sudden unexpected changes of plan in her methodical day.

Yes, all those reasons.

And....

The gastro-pub was perfect. Glamorous enough for the occasion, without being uncomfortably elegant. After they were seated and had ordered, Fiona began to relax. She fiddled with the stem of her wine glass, trying to stop herself drinking too quickly. She was suddenly starving.

'How's your dad these days?' Tony asked Spencer, leaning back in his chair. 'Got any exciting new projects on the horizon?'

'He's currently working on a new land acquisition deal - for another residential development, but it's hit a few stumbling blocks. Red tape, you know.'

'Right, right,' said Tony, nodding sagely.

Fiona wondered if her dad actually had any idea what the red tape might be.

'Is that the one where all the locals are writing nasty letters?' asked Nina.

Spencer made a face. He looked as if he didn't really want to get dragged into this conversation. 'Can't blame them. If it goes through, it'll make a pretty big impact on the village. I'd probably complain if I lived there.'

'Have you said that to your dad?' asked Fiona.

Spencer looked at her. 'We've spoken about it, yes.'

'But he doesn't agree?'

Spencer blew out his cheeks. 'It's a good deal. He stands to make a lot of money.' He looked suddenly helpless. 'Dad says if he doesn't do it, some other bugger will come along and snap it up. It'll get developed no matter what.'

'He probably has a point there,' said Tony.

'Yes, he does.' Spencer paused. 'But maybe the other bugger wouldn't be building only massive executive homes no-one in the area can afford! Maybe they would be building a decent range, with some starter homes, and some semis.' Spencer stopped and shook his head. 'Anyway, he'll do what he wants, he always does.'

'Men, eh?' said Nina.

'Hey, hey! Don't start on all that!' said Tony. 'This is the age of equality! You can't gang up on us. If we said, "Women, eh!" you'd be the first to complain about discrimination!'

'You say "Women, eh?" plenty of times!' Fiona pointed out.

'Shush!' said Tony, playfully.

'Shush?' repeated Nina in mock outrage. 'Did you hear that - male oppression!'

They all laughed. But, behind the laughter, Fiona wondered about Spencer and Spencer's dad, the snippets he'd mentioned about their relationship, and all the stuff which had been left unsaid.

While they were waiting for their desserts, Nina nipped off to find the toilets, and Tony got chatting to an old acquaintance at the bar.

Fiona sat across from Spencer, thinking how awkward this would have been a few months previously. Spencer was apparently thinking along the same lines.

'You know, I used to be really scared of you,' he said.

'What? Don't be daft.'

'Seriously. You're quite... Well, don't take this the wrong way, but you can be quite stand-offish - as a stranger I mean.'

'But you're Mr Laid Back! Nothing bothers you. I don't believe you were ever scared of me.'

'Wary then. I just didn't know how to talk to you.'

'Well, you've got over it!'

'Of course! I've had the chance to get to know you. And now I know how patient you are, and sensible.'

'God, I sound dreadfully dull!' said Fiona, staring into her wine glass morosely. She was aware of the effects of her third glass of wine; the unaccustomed blurring of her own edges.

'Not at all - what I'm trying to say is that I'm really pleased I've had the opportunity to get to know you as a person, and I now have complete faith in you. You're honest and generous and dedicated and hardworking. And you've taught me a lot - not just about riding. You're passionate about what you do - about giving the youngsters a chance. And when it matters - like with Echo - you're courageous.'

'Well, that's bollocks,' said Fiona, bitterly. 'When I so much as even think about riding into that ring, I'm a bag of nerves.'

'But you're still going to do it, aren't you?'

Fiona looked up at him. 'Yes.'

'I wish I could be that single minded.'

'About what?'

'About anything.'

'About telling your dad what you really think?'

Spencer studied her for a moment. 'Yes, about that.' He smiled and shook his head.

'What?'

'Nothing. You're just.... Can we add 'very astute' to the aforementioned qualities?'

Fiona sat on the edge of her bed, in the room which had been her room forever. Above her bed was a pinboard which held those faded rosettes from her childhood, a mass of old photos, and a few yellowing articles cut from newspapers and old horse magazines. She'd done nothing to update her room in years. It was, like her life, stagnant.

She'd kicked off the black heels, but was still wearing the dress. She felt strangely resistant to getting ready for bed; did not want to admit that the evening was over.

Nothing had happened. She went over and over the last few hours. She'd had too much wine, that was all. Her head was buzzing, her brain making up stuff that wasn't there.

When Nina had come back from the loo, she'd started talking straight away. Typical Nina. As though they'd just been sat there, waiting for her return to restart the conversation. And yet, whilst irritated, Fiona was relieved, because if Nina had been more observant, she might have noticed that it took a moment for Spencer to refocus, to pull back a little from the intensity of their conversation, to return to his habitual easy-going good humour.

She couldn't remember exactly what they had been talking about now. What she could remember was Spencer's expression - that light in his eyes when he was talking with enthusiasm and animation. The light in his eyes as they rested on her.

She put her head in her hands, rubbed her face.

Bloody Spencer.

'Sedgeworth, Friday after next,' said Tony, studying the laptop screen intently.

Fiona experienced a swooning feeling of sickness, shut her eyes, swallowed and said, 'OK, fine.'

'We're taking Rusty, so we can take the giraffe too.' Tony clicked something on the computer screen. 'You can both jump in the 6 year old class.'

'We'll be competing against one another?' said Fiona weakly.

Tony shrugged. 'Does it matter? Rusty has a chance to get in the money. This is a first time out for Echo, so think of it as a schooling round, get a bit of mileage under his belt.'

'Fine.' Fiona knew her dad half expected her to pull out on the day. Of course he wouldn't view Echo as any competition for Rusty.

Tony clicked to make the entries. 'You never know, might be lucky and someone will see him and make an offer.'

Fiona said nothing, but turned and walked away. The Friday after next she would be jumping at a show venue for the first time in over ten years.

The tack room was a sea of grey and burgundy. There were rugs, bandages and saddle cloths stacked up on the table in the corner.

'Blimey!' said Fiona.

'Great, isn't it?' Nina pulled a grey jacket from a bag, tried it on and did a twirl. It fitted like a glove, and looked fantastic. 'Nice, aren't they?'

'Really smart,' said Fiona.

'Glad you think so.' Nina reached behind her for another bag, and threw it across the room at her. 'I got you one too - now you're starting jumping again.'

Fiona goggled. She took out the beautiful jacket. It had a gorgeous burgundy-red lining, and a thin line of burgundy trim on the collar and over the pockets. She shrugged off her fleece, and tried on the jacket, then stood in front of the mirror which was screwed to the back of the door.

'There - you look like a proper rider now,' said Nina approvingly.

Fiona stood and stared at herself. It was indeed possible to believe that she was a hardened competition rider. She turned to Nina. 'Thank you.'

Nina shrugged. 'No probs. I just hope you get some wear out of it.'

Fiona stared at her reflection. She hoped so too.

There, I've done it. Fiona watched Spencer on Boris performing a working canter around the arena, his face set with determination. She pulled her phone out of her pocket and took a short video of them. He sat well in the saddle, no longer tipping forward, but sitting up, looking ahead, and keeping at one with the rhythm of the horse's movement. *I've done it. He can ride. Now we can stop this, and life can go back to normal.*

The relief was enormous. OK, underneath was something else. A devastating sense of loss and longing. But she was used to this. Loss and longing were part of her life.

She put the phone back in her pocket, watched Spencer bring Boris to a controlled trot and then to a walk. He gave Boris an enthusiastic pat, let him have a loose rein, and walked him over, grinning.

She began to clap, and grinned back at him, in spite of everything. 'Perfect!'

He swung down out of the saddle. Before she could react, he picked her up, spun her round and said, laughing, 'I bloody love you!'

Boris threw up his head and backed a pace. Spencer let go of Fiona, grabbed Boris's reins and said, 'Sorry chap.' He turned back to Fiona. 'That was brilliant.' His voice was rich with excitement and achievement.

Fiona was still reeling from the spin. She felt unbalanced, and not just physically. She heard her normal voice say, 'Congratulations on being the first - and last - person to graduate from the school of Fiona Castleton - rider first class!' But she felt as if she was floating above herself, observing herself in the third person.

They walked back to the yard together, Fiona continuing as a split person, both there in the moment, and the floating observer. Spencer talked non-stop, filling up the spaces where Fiona's thoughts should be, so that she had untacked Boris, brushed off his sweat marks and turned him out without even being aware of doing any of these things.

Spencer was still buzzing when he said his goodbyes and headed off. Fiona watched him climb into the little red Porsche (still grinning) and drive away.

Oh Spencer! *I bloody love you too.*

If she had been hoping anything would have changed in the last ten years, she knew now that she'd been kidding herself. The motion of the horse lorry travelling over the rutted car park of Sedgeworth Arena, the sight of all the other lorries and trailers parked up, the milling horses, the other competitors in their show gear, it was all exactly the same.

Fiona had been sick three times so far that morning. Twice before she'd even made it downstairs, and once when she'd come back in from the yard to get changed. Despite the fact it was physically impossible that there was anything left to bring up, she was pretty sure she was going to be sick again in the very near future.

One of the horses kicked the side of the lorry and whinnied sharply. It wasn't difficult to guess which one.

'Bloody hell,' Nina grumbled. 'Bet he's upset poor Rusty.'

Tony grunted. 'He'll get a bullet if he kicks a hole in the side of the lorry!' He swung the vehicle into the next available parking space, and silenced the engine. Fiona opened the passenger door and jumped gratefully to the ground. Her legs were wobbling.

Sophie's car pulled up beside them, and she immediately took over, pulling down the ramp, talking to the two horses.

Echo seemed to have grown en route. His head was thrown up, dangerously close to the roof of the box. Fiona went to untie him, while Sophie moved the partition, and Echo practically launched himself off the top of the ramp, dragging Fiona with him. He stood, dripping with sweat, trembling and blowing loudly at the bottom of the ramp, gazing at everything going on around him.

'Jesus!' said Nina. She fetched Rusty, who'd worked up a small sweat, but seemed otherwise unscathed, and tied him to the side of the lorry. It was clear they would not be able to do the same with Echo. Sophie kept him walking in small circles, while Fiona attempted to remove his travel boots.

'I'm going to confirm our entries,' said Nina. 'Or do you want to scratch?'

Fiona shook her head. 'Nope,' she said, grimly. 'We're here now.'

The warm-up ring was packed. Fiona could feel Echo still trembling beneath her, and he shied violently as a horse and rider came over the practise fence and swung dangerously close to them.

Another horse came up behind them, and Echo reared. As soon as all four feet were on the ground again, she sent him forward and worked him in a circle. From somewhere to her right she heard a voice say, 'Who's that on the roan?' and the answer, 'That's the other Castleton girl.'

This is ridiculous, she thought. Nodding to a steward, she and Echo slipped out of the ring and headed down the track away from the hubbub. She dimly remembered that back in the day there'd been a small flat area of grass where her mum had sometimes lunged the ponies for a couple of minutes if they were a bit fresh. Yes, there it was. A woman was hand-grazing a bay horse on the lush bank to one side, but otherwise the space was empty. Nodding an acknowledgement to the woman, Fiona began to work Echo. Circles and transitions, changes of rein, keeping him moving and not giving him time to think. Not giving herself time to think.

She had no idea how long it took, but finally Echo started to feel more like his usual self. He was listening to her, and his stride was even and full of spring. She glanced at her watch. Her class would have started. It was time to head back.

She kept her focus entirely on Echo, and did her best to ensure his was entirely on her. There were five horse and rider combinations in the warm-up arena. Echo's ears flicked as they went in, but she kept him moving, kept him working. They popped the practise fence as part of one of their circles, changed the rein, circled again to wait for another horse, popped the fence again, and came out.

And there was Spencer.

Her heart did a somersault.

'Not sure where Nina is - sorry!' she called, trying to keep Echo moving.

Spencer fell into step beside her. 'I didn't come for Nina, I came to support you.'

The nausea that Fiona had been fighting all morning rose up again. She took a gulping breath.

'Look, I can see I'm not helping, but I wanted to say I *know* you can do this.' He stood back. 'There are three more to go before you. Get in that collecting ring. You've got this.'

Fiona nodded at him but couldn't speak.

She turned away and rode towards the collecting ring.

She found she was hovering above herself again. Her gloved hands were on the reins, her legs wrapped around Echo's body, but she was also floating above, watching proceedings with interest. The minutes in the collecting ring seemed like hours, or seconds, she couldn't be sure. And then they were riding into the arena. Echo hesitated for a fraction of a second, but he responded when she pushed him on. *We have to do this.* She blocked out everything else - it was as though she had only the narrow field of vision in front of her. Just Echo's neck curving up between her hands. She gave him a pat, put him into canter and there was just the raw energy of him. The bell went, and they powered towards the first fence.

She did not remember the round. It happened so fast. Canter, take-off, suspension, landing, canter, turn, take-off. The jumps flew under his hooves. Then there was applause, and she was riding out of the arena. They had not touched a pole.

I'm in the jump off. I've got to do it again. But the blood was coursing through her veins now, and the thought was not so terrifying. She put her arms around Echo's neck and shut her eyes for a second. We bloody did it.

Someone was passing her a bottle of water. She took a swig, whilst registering it was Spencer. When she handed it back to him, he squeezed her hand.

'You were brilliant.'

She squeezed his hand back, then let go and rode on. Her heart was full to bursting.

She walked Echo down to the grass area and back twice. On her second return journey, Sophie ran up to her.

'Nina's gone clear too. They've just published the jump off course. Go and look. I'll hold him.'

It struck Fiona that she'd not done this - this having to memorise the jump off course. Not for years. A sudden memory flashed into her brain of being tiny, standing holding her mum's hand, her mum explaining to her that she didn't need to jump the red and white or the one with the filler in the shape of a smiling pig. She needed to turn instead, really quickly, and gallop straight for the green and white poles.

Hope you're still with me, mum. She studied the course. Saw a gamble between fences three and four, and another between six and seven. Echo was a big striding horse, but he was nimble too. It was possible. Just.

As they circled again in the warm-up, she could hear poles falling, the spectators gasp and groan. Later, a smattering of applause. After that, she was not aware of anything at all. The only way she could manage this was to focus on Echo.

She moved into the collecting ring. From the side, Sophie gave her a thumbs up, and then she was riding into the arena for the second time.

Even while he was in the air over fence three, Fiona was shifting her weight, turning Echo left, so that he landed, turned and took the next stride all in one fluid movement. Fence four flashed beneath them, and on they went. At six, she did the same again, this time turning right, and again, he saw immediately what she wanted, and reached for the stride. They just touched fence seven, but nothing fell, and they galloped on. Only when they'd jumped the final fence and flashed through the timing device did she hear the applause. Her eyes blurred with tears. Double clear. A double clear!

She rode out, slid to the floor, threw her arms around Echo's neck and cried. The relief of it, the overwhelming relief of having done it was almost too much. Echo stood, sides heaving from the effort, but no longer afraid.

Sophie appeared. 'Bloody brilliant!' she grinned. 'Nina's warming up. I'll take Echo - you go and watch the other rounds.'

Fiona slipped into the edge of the seating area and stood with a couple of other riders watching the current round in progress.

A girl said, 'Well done - fantastic jump off round, yours. Genius, going inside those two fences.'

Fiona flashed her a grateful smile. 'Thanks! But I bet everyone else did it too!'

The girl looked at her strangely. 'No - some have tried - but no.'

The horse in the ring brought down fence seven, and a guy standing nearby grimaced and turned away.

The girl nodded at the results display. 'You're still the fastest clear.'

Fiona stared at the score board in disbelief.

An arm came round her, squeezed and then let go.

Spencer.

'Well done, you!' he whispered in her ear.

A warm glow rose up within her. The glow of success. And of something else - the joy of Spencer's praise.

Nina rode into the ring on Rusty.

'And last to go,' said the commentator, 'Nina Castleton on Soldier's Gold.'

There was a ripple of applause from the audience; someone whooped. Nina was so well known here. She looked poised and perfect as usual. Rusty's coat gleamed and, taking a couple of rein back steps, he went into a smooth canter.

The first five fences were text book and fast. Just like Fiona, Nina went for the turn between three and four and it paid off. She was a nano-second faster.

She'll beat me, of course thought Fiona. But it didn't really matter. She'd already achieved what she'd set out to do.

At fence six, she could see Nina pushing Rusty on strongly, there was a moment's hesitation and then he was in the air. Nina was clearly going for the same turn, but in trying to cut the corner, Rusty clipped the back pole. It came crashing down.

The spectators let out a collective groan.

Fiona spun round to gaze at Spencer, a jubilant smile on her face. She'd done it! She'd beaten Nina!

And then there was a sickening crash of poles, and a collective gasp of horror.

Spencer was staring at the ring, the colour draining from his face, and when Fiona turned to look, there was Rusty scrambling to his feet, and Nina lying inert in a tangle of poles.

Life was brutal. Even when you got what you wished for, it had to twist the knife.

Fiona sat in the passenger seat of the Porsche, and counted the things which had only a short time ago seemed so important. She'd competed with Echo. She had won her class. She had beaten her sister. Spencer had come to support her. And she was now sitting beside him in his sports car.

Tick, tick, tick, tick, tick. And yet, it had all been obliterated in a single second. The image of Nina, lying so still in the mess of fallen poles, made her feel sick with fear.

Now they were on the way to the hospital. Tony had gone in the Ambulance. Sophie had stayed to take care of the horses. A friend of Tony's had offered to drive the box back to the yard.

Spencer drove in silence, every ounce of concentration on the road. He was holding his bottom lip between his teeth. His hands moved deftly to change gear, to indicate, to overtake the slow vehicle in front. He had said nothing the whole journey. As a result neither had Fiona.

She wondered if he felt he had somehow overstepped the mark with her. Wondered if he was regretting the casual arm around her waist, the joking way he'd once told her he loved her. Perhaps it all seemed crass and stupid now.

They turned into the hospital entrance, followed signs for A&E, and found a space in the car park. He was out of the car before her, but he waited without meeting her eye, clicked the central locking, and headed towards the main doors.

Tony was waiting inside. He looked to have aged ten years in the last hour.

'They've taken her to ICU. She hadn't regained consciousness. They're worried about swelling on the brain.'

Spencer blanched.

'But she was wearing a helmet,' Fiona protested.

'One of the poles hit her straight in the face,' said Tony.

Another wave of sickness washed over Fiona; she shut her eyes and waited for it to pass. 'So, what - we just wait?'

Tony nodded. He was ahead of her, processing this information. He was quiet now.

'Shall I get you both a coffee?' Spencer gestured towards the machine in the corner.

Fiona nodded. Tony made an almost imperceptible shrugging movement.

So there it was. After all the rushing, now there was only the interminable wait, sipping hot brown liquid from plastic cups.

After some time had passed - minutes or hours, Fiona wasn't sure - Tony stood up with difficulty, said he was going out for some air, and limped off out through the doors.

Spencer, his elbows on his knees, hunched forward and ran his hands through his hair.

Neither of them said anything.

Guilt and love hung over them like a sodden blanket.

Fiona huddled under her duvet, not sleeping, snippets from the day filtering through her mind. When they'd left, Nina was still in an induced coma. Spencer had dropped them off at home, Tony in the front seat of the Porsche, Fiona wedged into the tiny backseat. They said they'd ring each other if there was any news. She was dreading the kind of news that needed to be shared in the middle of the night.

She'd imagined every possible outcome. Nina dying. Spencer going out of her life forever. Tony, all the spirit crushed out of him, sitting in his chair for the rest of his days, dosed up on painkillers. Everything feeling utterly pointless. Nina brain-damaged. Fiona giving up the yard and all the horses. Working round the clock to care for her brain-damaged sibling. Spencer sticking around for a while, gradually visiting less and less frequently, then disappearing altogether. Nina recovering - wanting nothing to do with horses ever again. Marrying Spencer. Fiona and Spencer skirting around each other for the rest of their days, pushing to the back of their minds that once they had been on the verge of -

What exactly?

Finally, she fell asleep. And dreamed that Spencer asked her to marry him while Nina was still unconscious. And the ceremony was performed in the arena at Sedgworth with the spectators booing them, and a voice saying, 'He was supposed to marry *Nina* Castleton - not the other Castleton girl.'

She rang the hospital first thing in the morning. Nina had had a 'comfortable' night, but there was no change. Fiona took a cup of tea up to her dad and told him to stay in bed a little longer. She texted Spencer while she walked down to the yard. She couldn't face ringing him.

The horses whinnied for their breakfasts, but even they were subdued. Boris did not even kick his door.

She reduced all the horses' breakfast feeds, then turned out and mucked out. She'd told Sophie to take the morning off since she'd had such a long day the previous day. She was glad of the work, and the solitude.

She drove Tony to the hospital mid-morning. Spencer was standing in the corridor outside the ICU, and at first she thought there'd been a turn for the worst - he looked so ashen. But he explained he'd just had to come out for some air - it was so hot in there. He looked shame-faced. 'All that she's having to go through, and I can't even sit by her bedside without feeling queasy!' he said bitterly.

Fiona wanted to reach out and hold him but she stood, still and mute, hating herself.

In the ICU, Nina could have only two visitors at a time, so for a while Tony and Fiona sat together, watching Nina silently. The bruising on her face was coming out now - livid and blue - and her whole face was puffy. Fiona gazed at the tubes and the monitors without truly knowing if the various beeps were good beeps or something to be alarmed about.

Eventually Tony shook his head, pushed himself to his feet and walked out.

Alone with Nina, Fiona stroked her hand and said, 'I don't know if you can hear me, but I've got a confession. I've been teaching Spencer to ride - he wanted it to be a surprise, so we didn't tell you. He was pretty rubbish to begin with, but - well, I think you'll be pretty impressed now. He can trot and canter and he looks pretty good in the saddle. In fact, if you hurry up and wake up, I can show you a video.' She paused. The machines continued to bleep, but there was no change in Nina. 'The thing is,' Fiona went on, 'he was dead nervous to begin with - thought he was going to come off all the time. But because he loves you, he was determined to keep going. And because he loves you, he did it. So you see, you've got to get better. Because he loves you that much. You see?'

She couldn't say any more, because tears had started tumbling down her cheeks and were clogging up her throat.

She felt, rather than heard, a movement behind her and turned. Spencer was staring at her. She couldn't read his expression, but he was clearly in pain. His own eyes were misty with tears.

There, she thought. There, I've said it for the both of us.

She gave him a watery smile, but he didn't smile back.

Sunday was a long day with no change. In the evening, she'd made dinner even though Tony professed not to be hungry. She herself was starving, but admitting to being so seemed like another thing to feel guilty about.

Sophie had done the horses in the morning, and turned all of them out again. Fiona did evening feeds and brought in Rusty, Echo and Boris, leaving all the youngsters out. Rusty was apparently unscathed from his fall. There'd been a bit of heat in one foreleg on the first day, but nothing more. Even so, she preferred having him in.

Echo was like a different horse since his day competing - calm and relaxed around the yard. If she'd had any emotion left inside her, Fiona would have been proud of him.

There'd been a raft of phone messages and emails from people asking after Nina. She did her best to answer them, but had so little to say.

When she woke on Monday, there was a moment where she couldn't remember what was wrong. Then the weight of it hit her afresh. She phoned the hospital (no change) fed the horses, turned out and mucked out. When she got back to the kitchen, the postman had been. There was a small jiffy bag addressed to her, and an envelope addressed to Nina.

She opened the jiffy bag. A red rosette fell out onto the kitchen table. She ran her finger tips over the ribbon, over the cardboard centre disk with the gold writing proclaiming her First. Someone at Sedgeworth must have posted it on automatically because she'd not stayed to collect it.

A red rosette. Tick.

Tears sprang into her eyes again. She stuffed the rosette back in the jiffy bag and stuck it in the kitchen drawer.

She wiped her hands across her eyes and texted Spencer. He texted back saying he would drive them over to the hospital. She assumed he was borrowing his dad's car again, but when a nondescript silver hatchback turned up in the drive, she was taken aback.

'Porsche in the garage or something?' she asked.

'Or something,' said Spencer, grimly.

Fiona looked at him.

'I sold it.'

'What? I thought you loved that car.'

He shrugged. 'There's a whole load of other stuff which is more important. You taught me that.'

'What do you mean?'

'I had that conversation with my dad.'

'I don't understand.'

At that moment, Tony appeared in the doorway. 'More sensible vehicle,' he said, eyeing the hatchback. 'I've got a fighting chance of getting into this one!'

Spencer looked at Fiona across the roof of the car. 'I'll explain later.'

'So you told him you didn't want to be involved with the scheme anymore?'

They sat across from each other at a small square table in the hospital cafeteria, both clutching coffees in tall cardboard cups.

'Yup, after that meal, I thought about what we talked about, what you said. I decided to confront him with my opinion. I tried to reason with him,' said Spencer. 'I showed him I'd worked it all out - how many starter homes, how many terraces, how many semis, and just a couple of the flag ship four and five beds which he wanted. I'd done the plans and the figures. It made financial sense and they all fitted into the same footprint.'

'Did he even bother to look?'

'Oh yes, he looked.'

'And?'

'He just laughed. He said I was wet behind the ears and knew nothing.' Spencer's face twisted with suppressed fury. 'And I could have taken that if I'd not done the prep work - but I had. I'd worked it all out. My figures were right. And he knew it. What he couldn't stand was that it was my idea, and he hadn't thought of it.'

'Wow.'

'So I said I no longer wanted to work with him or for him. And he laughed at that too and said he'd like to see me last for five minutes without his money.'

Fiona blew out her cheeks. 'I know he's your dad and everything, but he sounds like a bit of a wanker.'

'Oh yes, he's definitely that.' Spencer took a swig of his coffee. 'Mum went mad, started wailing at him that he was driving me away, and telling me not to overreact.'

'So you decided to not overreact by selling the Porsche?'

'Yup. Put the Porsche up for sale, put a deposit on a little flat, and put in an application for a job with a rival firm.' He paused. 'I'd planned to tell you all this after the show - but obviously, things didn't quite go to plan. The guy came to pick up the Porsche yesterday. Oh yeah, and all my worldly possessions are in the boot of the hatchback.'

'Do you need somewhere to stay tonight?'

Spencer gazed at her. 'I was going to stay with a friend, but I rather get the impression his girlfriend isn't keen, so...'

'We've got a spare bedroom,' said Fiona. 'It's yours for as long as you need it.'

Her phone, lying on the table, suddenly vibrated.

'Dad?' she said.

'She's awake!' said Tony's voice. 'Come up now! She's just woken up.'

The hospital said they wanted to keep Nina in for another couple of days for observation. She was still groggy, and there was still a lot of swelling. But she was also most definitely still Nina; cussing and muttering about the pain, about how bad the appalling swelling looked, how rubbish it was not being allowed to drink anything other than water.

'I don't think they do a Pinot Grigio drip!' said Fiona, grinning at her fondly.

'Oh don't!' she groaned. 'My head is banging like I've been on a three day bender!'

Fiona couldn't believe how much joy she felt from listening to her little sister moaning and whinging again. She didn't believe she would ever be sick of it again.

Spencer was hovering in the foyer.

'Come on dad, let's give these two some privacy,' said Fiona. 'I'll take you downstairs for a cuppa.'

'I'd prefer a blooming Scotch!' Tony muttered, hoisting himself up.

'Blimey, the staff in here will think we're all alcoholics!' Fiona winked at Nina, put her arm around her dad's shoulders and gave Spencer the bravest smile she could muster. There was a stab of pain as she saw him take her place in the seat at Nina's bedside, smiling earnestly at her, but it was nothing in comparison with the joy of having Nina back.

It was four more days before Nina came home, carried into the lounge in Spencer's tanned arms.

Fiona fussed around her, got her a blanket and a drink, a pile of magazines, some grapes. Made sure the remote control for the telly was nearby.

'I could get used to this!' said Nina.

'Don't!' said Fiona, darkly.

'By the way, I never said - congratulations! That was a hell of a round!'

Fiona grinned and shook her head. 'Didn't think you'd

remember.'

'Course I remember! That's why I was riding like a mad thing, trying to beat you! Can't believe I didn't make it. Where's your rosette? Hope it's on the pinboard!'

Fiona thought of the rosette, stuffed ignominiously into the kitchen drawer. 'No, but it will be.' That reminded her of the envelope for Nina. She went to fetch it.

'Blimey - these are the photo shoot pictures. Look!' Nina slid out the glossy prints. Nina in all the grey and burgundy clobber. Nina standing with the horses in their rugs. Nina sitting on Rusty. She looked like a super model.

'They'll have to airbrush out my broken nose in the future!' said Nina ruefully.

'You can barely notice now the swelling has gone down,' said Fiona. 'Don't worry - you're still beautiful.'

Nina looked at her out of the top of her eyes. 'That's what the doctor said!'

'Oh yes?'

Nina grinned at her coyly.

When Fiona went out to the yard later, she could hear an engine and a rattling-chinking sound. When she went to investigate, Tony was chain harrowing the top paddock, sitting on the old quadbike. She was slightly more taken aback to find Spencer, stripped to the waist, nailing on some new fence rails.

'I thought dad was getting someone in to do the fencing.'

'He has - me!' said Spencer, grinning sheepishly. 'He's a bit of a slave driver.'

'Tell me about it!' said Fiona. She didn't quite know where to look.

'I'm working my board and lodging!'

'You don't have to!'

'I want to.' He shrugged. 'Besides, it's good - this kind of manual work. I mean, I've done bits on the building sites, but this is nicer. In the fields, watching the horses, listening to the birds.'

'Or the chain harrow?'

'Yup, that too.' He paused, looked down and back up again. 'And knowing you're there, in the yard or in the house or whatever.'

The world tipped out of kilter again. Fiona had only just got used to life being back to normal.

'Don't,' she said.

'Don't what? Tell you how I feel? You must know!' He looked at her steadily.

'What about Nina?'

He took a breath. 'Nina and I have had a lot of good conversations in the last couple of days. And we're always going to be friends. But...we've agreed to go our separate ways. It was funny - she was worried about letting me down gently and I was worried about letting her down gently. Turns out, she's got a bit of a crush on her doctor! Plus, I get the impression I'm not quite as much of a catch now I'm no longer the heir to a massive fortune!' He made a face. 'I'm just hoping you don't feel the same way.'

Fiona stepped towards the fence. 'Quite the opposite.'

'Good.' Spencer put down the hammer, reached for her hands and said, 'So does that mean you'll let me take you for lunch now.'

'No.' She shook her head solemnly.

'What? Why?' Spencer's face clouded with dismay.

'Because you haven't got any money,' said Fiona with a grin. She leaned towards him and placed a soft kiss on his lips. 'But how about I treat you?'

THE END

ACKNOWLEDGEMENTS

Terrified Tuesdays was first published in the Woman's Weekly Fiction Special in March 2015, and *The Companion Pony* was first published (as *'If Wishes Were Horses'*) in The People's Friend 2016 Annual. I'm grateful to both magazines for their support of the short story genre in the UK.

Thank you to all the amazing people I have met through a shared love of horses, especially those who have talked to me about this project, and told me their own stories - you have all inspired me. Thanks also to my husband Paul for allowing me to (indeed sometimes making me) go to my writing room for hours on end - and for putting up with my inattention when my head was still in a story.

Lol Jones Photography deserves a special mention for the beautiful image which features on the cover, as does Shar at itsawrapdesigns.com who was ever patient with my indecision during the design process.

And thank you to the members of my long-suffering writers' group for their support, encouragement, and advice on all these stories (and many others!). Special thanks to Claire Weatherhead, Sue Hancocks, Mark Pearce and Emma Hancox for helping to ensure the text didn't turn out to be complete nonsense.

ABOUT THE AUTHOR

Jenny Roman used to be a ponyless, pony mad kid gazing longingly at other people's horses, but didn't get her own pony until she reached the age of 28! She's had all kinds of jobs to support her equine habit - including working at a riding school, and as a painter and decorator.

Jenny had her first short story published in PONY magazine when she was a teenager, and has since written short stories and articles for a variety of magazines. She has an MA in Creative Writing from Nottingham Trent University, and has been a story competition judge. She is a member of a Writers' Group and strongly recommends this to anyone thinking of writing creatively.

Now she's a grown-up(ish), she is lucky enough to have a beautiful horse of her own, and lives with her husband and two dogs in rural Shropshire, enjoying the country life.

IF YOU ENJOYED THESE STORIES

Sign up for Jenny Roman's newsletter
and get a short story delivered to your inbox absolutely FREE:

http://bit.ly/JennyRomanNewsletter

Printed in Great Britain
by Amazon

13602639R00103